Assessing Community Strengths

Other Titles in this Series

Assessing Community Strengths

A practical handbook for planning capacity building

by Steve Skinner and Mandy Wilson

COMMUNITY DEVELOPMENT FOUNDATION
• PUBLICATIONS •

First Published in Great Britain in 2002 by the
Community Development Foundation
60 Highbury Grove
London N5 2AG
Registered charity number 306130

British Library Cataloguing-in-Publication Data
A record of this publication is available from the British Library.

ISBN 1 901974 31 6

Cover design and Typesetting by Bears Communications, Amsterdam
Printed in Great Britain by Crowes Complete Print, Norwich

The Joseph Rowntree Foundation has supported this project as part of its programme of research and development projects, which it hopes will be of value to policy makers, practitioners and service users. The facts presented and views expressed in this report, however, are those of the author and not necessarily those of the Foundation, nor are they necessarily those of the publisher, the Community Development Foundation.

Community Development Foundation

The Community Development Foundation (CDF) is a non-departmental public body supported by the Active Community Unit of the Home Office. Its role is to pioneer, study and promote new forms of community development, in order to inform public policy, professional practice and community initiatives.

Set up in 1968, CDF strengthens communities by ensuring the effective participation of people in determining the conditions which affect their lives. A leading authority on community development and associated issues in the UK and mainland Europe, CDF works through:

- local action projects
- development of best practice
- research, evaluation and policy analysis
- consultancies and training programmes
- conferences and seminars
- information and publications.

CDF provides services to, and works in partnership with, public, private, community and voluntary organisations.

Community Development Foundation, 60 Highbury Grove, London, N5 2AG
Tel: 020 7226 5375; *Fax*: 020 7704 0313; *Email*: admin@cdf.org.uk
Website: www.cdf.org.uk

Contents

Preface

These guidelines describe how a community strengths assessment can be carried out to find out about the strengths and needs of community and voluntary organisations. They also describe how to determine the level of community strengths and decide on future action. The guidelines include:

- practical ideas on how to produce a profile, taking you step by step through what's involved

- ready-made questions that you can use and adapt to survey the needs of groups in your community

- a Community Strengths Framework to help to interpret and make use of the information collected

- proposals on using this approach as a planning tool in regeneration programmes and capacity building initiatives

- reference to other books and publications as a further resource.

The material for this handbook comes from a new approach to community profiling developed by the Department of Community Development and Life Long Learning of Bradford Council, working jointly with COGS. The survey was piloted in Bradford, with contributions to its development from many different groups and organisations.

This approach is based on the belief that real, lasting change in communities happens at the grass roots and that strong, well-organised community organisations are the building blocks for new projects, partnerships and local action. Community strengths assessments are essential for effective planning of regeneration programmes and to ensure capacity building initiatives are based on a proper assessment of groups' needs. This handbook can help to ensure communities are able to be fully involved in achieving real change.

Steve Skinner, Mandy Wilson
February 2002

Acknowledgements

The authors would like to thank the following for their support in the production of this handbook.

The Bradford New Deal for Communities Partnership
This handbook is based on a major case study of a community strengths profile carried out in Bradford's New Deal for Communities area. The authors would like to thank the many community workers, agencies and groups in this area, as well as the Bradford Trident partnership, that have actively supported the work.

Bradford Capacity Building Project
This innovative project consisted of a team of capacity builders who were working throughout the Bradford Objective Two area. Members of the team were involved in carrying out the survey work for the pilots in Horton Grange and the New Deal for Communities area.

The Joseph Rowntree Foundation (JRF)
JRF is a trust based in York that funds an extensive programme of research and projects in the field of regeneration and social policy. The Foundation financially assisted the production of the handbook and organised an Advisory Group.

The Allerton Health Project, Bradford
This locally-based project organised the survey work for the community strengths profile pilot on the Allerton and Lower Grange estates. Debbie, Juliette and Gloria, the three community researchers, gave a lot of their time and energy. The pilot was also supported by the Barnardo's Community Scheme, Allerton.

South Yorkshire Objective One Programme
The community strengths framework is based on a model developed by COGS for the South Yorkshire Objective One Priority 4 Driver Partnership and built on initial ideas from the South Yorkshire Community and Voluntary Sector Open Forum members. The Objective One Programme Directorate and the Open Forum have allowed the framework to be used and developed.

COGS (Communities and Organisations: Growth and Support)
Pete Wilde, the COGS Consultant, who with Mandy Wilson, developed and designed the initial framework. Thanks also to Annie Rosewarne, COGS Associate.

The Community Development Policy Unit, Bradford Council
The CDPU is based in the Department of Community Development and Life Long Learning. Staff within the unit contributed a lot of their time and expertise in designing and organising the pilots in Bradford.

Laing Partnership Housing
Laing have generously contributed to the costs of publishing *Assessing Community Strengths*.

The following people provided helpful support, advice and guidance: Kevin Maxim, Chas Stansfield and Steve Hartley, Bradford Trident; Trudi Wilson, Pat Fairfax, Nigel Smith, Mick Charlton, Bob Adsett, Phil Baldwin, Mick Binns and Joyce Thacker, City of Bradford Metropolitan District Council; Terry Allen, University of Bradford; Maria Kane, NCVO; Anthony Clipsom, Bradford Council for Voluntary Service; Murray Hawtin and Andrew Petrie, Policy Research Institute, Leeds; Tony Herrman and Alan Anderton, Community Work Training Company; Ranjit Kaur, QED; Professor Peter Lloyd, Liverpool University; Geoff Needham, Yorkshire Forward; Sheila Philpott, Bushara Anjam Ali, Kevin Metcalfe, Anna Frater and Paul Hamilton, Bradford Capacity Building Project; John Routledge, Urban Forum; Helen Thompson, Yorkshire and Humberside Voluntary and Community Sector Regional Forum; David Wilcox, Freelance Consultant; Katherine Wyatt, The Joint Training Board, Bradford; Gabriel Chanan and Alison Gilchrist, Community Development Foundation.

Special thanks to all the people who took part in the surveys, workshops and focus groups.

Introduction to community strengths assessments

Introduction to Community Strengths Assessments

Community profiles and audits are often used to provide key information on a number of crucial local issues:

- social needs and problems, such as employment levels, drug abuse and housing conditions

- facilities, such as libraries, sports clubs and public buildings

- local services, such as shops, social services, health provision

- plans for the future development of the area.

Such profiles and audits have a crucial role to play in regeneration and community development, and several very useful publications are available that describe how to carry them out.

A community strengths assessment, however, is different. It focuses particularly on the community and voluntary groups in an area and looks at how they are organised, what their aims and needs are, what support they are getting and what support they might need in future.

A community strengths assessment will be useful for:

- assessing the level of community organisation, either in a neighbourhood or in a community of interest

- planning support for community groups, through capacity building and community development initiatives

- providing baseline information for regeneration programmes concerning the potential for joint working and community involvement

- establishing neighbourhood management and community-based projects.

In some areas communities may be poorly organised and need basic community development support to help get things moving. Other areas may already have many well-established community groups and voluntary organisations, but need more specialist help so that people can be more involved in running local projects and in managing regeneration initiatives.

Assessing community strengths will be useful in any area, not just those areas involved in regeneration programmes and neighbourhood renewal. For example, the process may be useful for local community planning or for informing the development of district-wide strategies. The key feature is that community strengths assessments can provide a systematic description of the baseline of community capacity by focusing on the needs and strengths of community and voluntary groups. The approach to assessing community strengths we take in this book includes the following stages and elements:

- a survey of community and voluntary groups – described in Part Two

- a survey of organisations providing support to community and voluntary groups – described in Part Three

- the process of analysing and interpreting the information gathered – described in Part Four

- applying the resulting community strengths framework at workshops and focus groups to check out the findings and collectively agree on the current level of development – described in Part Five

- planning for action and future development, and where appropriate devising a capacity building strategy – described in Part Six.

Materials to assist you through each of these stages are included in the resources section in Part Seven.

In summary, then, the process of assessing community strengths involves both carrying out a community strengths profile (described in Parts Two to Four) and applying the Community Strengths Framework (described in Part Five with additional material in Parts Six and Seven).

The main stages in a community strengths assessment

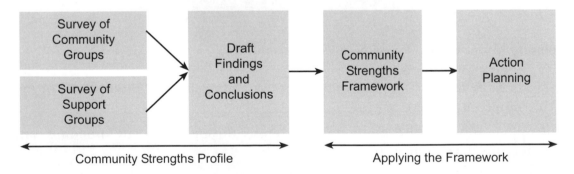

The role of community strengths assessments

This section focuses on the potential use of community strengths assessments. Community strengths assessments have a role to play in a range of contexts. Some of the main ones include:

- planning local projects and initiatives

- setting up neighbourhood renewal and regeneration programmes

- community planning
- tackling social exclusion
- understanding and networking between community groups
- joint working and partnerships between communities and agencies.

Planning local projects and initiatives

Building a picture of community strengths is a useful resource for any community – it can provide a firm basis for designing new local projects, for preparing funding bids and devising local action plans. Community strengths assessments are an important tool for communities to describe their own area and, along with other information, present their own case for action and new developments. Community strengths assessments have a key role to play in any community – not just in regeneration areas or other programme initiatives.

Setting up neighbourhood renewal and regeneration programmes

Setting up and running effective regeneration programmes require community involvement and leadership so that local authorities and agencies can work in partnership with local people. Research and experience from Single Regeneration Budget (SRB) and European-funded development programmes (Lloyd, 1996) illustrates that neighbourhoods at a very low baseline of community organisation may require assistance to help build skills and structures in order to more fully participate in regeneration initiatives. At the start of a regeneration programme of neighbourhood renewal initiatives, some areas may be well placed to respond to new opportunities while others may require an initial period of support and development work. Community strengths assessments could consequently provide a systematic baseline position of the potential for community participation and leadership, and identify gaps that need to be addressed through capacity building initiatives. Community strengths assessments will also specifically have a role to play in neighbourhood renewal. The National Strategy for Neighbourhood Renewal's main aim is to bring deprived areas up to the national average in specific economic and social indicators (Social Exclusion Unit, 2000). Neighbourhood management is seen as a key way to reach these targets, by bringing together public, private, community and voluntary sector bodies to co-ordinate services and initiatives on an area basis. Neighbourhood management, suggests the report, needs to be led by or at least influenced by the community with core public services investing in building community capacity. A thorough assessment of existing community capacity will need to be carried out as part of such initiatives.

Assessing community strengths could consequently influence and guide the type of programme designed – this point is explored in more detail in Part Six on Planning for Action.

Community planning

Part One of the Local Government Act 2000 placed local authorities under a duty to prepare a community strategy for promoting the social, environmental and economic wellbeing of their areas. Community strategies aim to identify local actions that will improve the quality of life for all sections of the community, based on a long-term vision. Such a vision, to achieve lasting impact, will need to be based on the reality of the baseline starting point for communities in each city/district. Local strategic partnerships will need to be pro-active in ensuring communities are involved in the planning process and that the capacity for effective involvement and partnership working is assessed. This issue is discussed more fully in Part Five.

Tackling social exclusion

This leads on to the wider issue of how more marginalised sections of the community are given the opportunity to participate in the mainstream and benefit from services and resources on an equal basis. Community strengths assessments can also be carried out on the basis of communities of interest or identity rather than on the basis of area. For example, a profile could be built of African–Caribbean community organisations spread across a whole district. Such profiles could usefully inform district-wide community strategies (DETR, 2000). See Part Six for further information on this potential use.

Understanding and networking between community groups

Communities are made up of diverse and often hidden groups and interests. Community strengths profiles can help to increase local knowledge about what is happening and where, what support is available and for what. This knowledge also enhances opportunities for developing contacts and networking with others. It helps to identify and measure the combined strengths of local groups and create a common vision. For example, the information gathered through the profile could be used to produce a comprehensive local directory of community and voluntary organisations.

Joint working and partnerships between communities and agencies

A new climate is developing where in order to tackle inequalities and improve services, local authorities and other public agencies increasingly want to work jointly with local communities. For local authorities, initiatives such as Best Value, Modernising Local Government and Local Agenda 21 call for increased consultation and involvement. Equally many health service organisations are looking to the voluntary and community sector to work jointly with them in achieving nationally-set targets concerning health inequalities. Many funding bodies will want to know what the potential is for joint working and how geared up local community groups are to take on new projects and initiatives. Community strengths assessments can help to identify the starting point for effective joint working.

The origins of this publication

In 2000, Bradford Council worked jointly with COGS to devise a new approach to assessing community strengths. This handbook draws on pilots carried out in three different parts of Bradford, with many local projects and groups contributing to this initiative. In particular, the experience gained from the profile carried out in the New Deal for Communities area is described as a major case study throughout this publication. An early version of the community groups questionnaire was first designed by the Community Development Foundation for use in the Sandwell District, West Midlands, in combination with a household survey. The approach used in this earlier work is described in Part Seven, Resource Six. The community strengths framework has been developed from an original model developed by COGS for South Yorkshire Objective One Priority 4 Driver Partnership (COGS, 2000a). The creation of this handbook has drawn on all these different sources.

The main features of this approach

Community strengths profiles are an innovative form of assessment of community capacity. Our approach is based on a set of principles and elements – which we now discuss. We go on to describe what the approach is not attempting to do!

- **Community strengths profiles are mainly about community and voluntary groups, and not particularly about individuals.** Community strengths profiles are primarily about the collective activities of community and voluntary groups. The needs, skills and role of individuals will obviously contribute to the community development and regeneration initiatives in the area. The focus here, however, is on the needs and potential role of community groups and organisations, with individuals' needs being addressed within this context. In other words, in community strengths profiles, building effective community involvement and leadership is seen as being primarily identified through the collective activity of local community and voluntary groups.

- **Community strengths profiles emphasise the importance of the grass roots.** Too often in regeneration programmes and the design of new projects, only the larger voluntary sector organisations are consulted or involved. The approach used in community strength profiles, however, is to emphasise the importance of smaller community and voluntary groups. The survey is designed to actively include these grass-roots groups and ensures their needs are considered. The needs of these grass-roots groups are included because, in terms of effective regeneration, they are the bedrock of healthy communities and the potential for lasting change. Our approach also emphasises strengths of communities – too often the picture painted of neighbourhoods focuses exclusively on problems, the indicators of deprivation – rather than what communities have to offer and contribute to the renewal process.

- **The profile contains two main elements – level of community organisation and level of support.** Both these elements, introduced and described in Part One, need to be assessed to establish a clear baseline of community capacity. An area may have a reasonable degree of community organisation but lack effective support for it to develop further. Equally the surveys may reveal a low level of community organisation despite an apparently high level of support, which would indicate the support infrastructure is not addressing local needs effectively. Part Five presents a framework that can be used to establish a broad assessment of the levels of strength of different areas in terms of these two key elements. In combination, these two elements will help to build a comprehensive picture of a neighbourhood and highlight gaps in both activity and infrastructure that can be acted on through new initiatives and planning.

- **The approach is based on community development principles**. Community development values underpin the approach used in this handbook. These values include social justice, participation, equality, learning and co-operation. Our approach draws heavily on a model of community development called ABCD – Achieving Better Community Development (see Barr and Hashagen, 2000 a, b and c). ABCD has been used extensively across the UK and has had active support from government departments. It identifies community development as being crucially concerned with the process of community empowerment. This in turn can be understood through four key dimensions – personal empowerment, positive action, community organisation, involvement and participation. These four dimensions have been adapted for use in community strengths profiles and renamed in this handbook as Building skills, Building organisation, Building equality and Building involvement.

A strategic approach to community development:

'• recognises and analyses the changing context
- is about working with communities in ways which are empowering, educating and enabling
- ensures that resources are accessible and allocated fairly within and between communities
- has clear processes for evaluation and dissemination
- links community development with strategies for learning
- ensures that organisations across sectors have policies and practices which support quality community development
- encourages involvement in existing networks and the creation of new networks to support the strategy.'

SCCD, 2001, p. 22.

The main limits of this approach

In this Introduction, the aim has been to clarify the potential roles of community strengths assessments so that they can be carried out effectively. The profile method and framework – which in combination form a community strengths assessment – are primarily tools to assess the level of community capacity. In this publication community capacity has been named 'community strengths' because this is a more positive – and less patronising – term. Community strengths assessments have a particular role and it is worth being clear what it is not trying to cover:

- **Community strengths profiles are not attempting to assess the extent to which community and voluntary groups serve the needs of the people living in a neighbourhood**. Assessing this would involve examining in some detail the nature and level of use by the local population of such groups' services and activities. It would need a household survey to be carried out to identify the pattern of use and involvement. Community strengths profiles are not designed to address this issue. Such a household-based survey could be carried out in parallel to a community strengths profile and would form a useful complement. This approach was successfully developed in studies in Sandwell, West Midlands, in work carried out by the Community Development Foundation in 1996–97. These studies are summarised in Part 6 of the resource section. In some cases it will be useful to combine the two methods to develop a fully comprehensive approach to assessing both community capacity and community activity. The Sandwell study is being produced as a companion publication to the present handbook (Dale and Humm, 2002).

- **Community strengths assessments are not intended primarily as an evaluation framework for community development.** The ABCD model, described briefly above, serves this purpose. It is however, from ABCD that the community strengths profile and framework have been developed, and certainly community strengths assessments could form a useful part of a wider evaluation of community development where a specific evaluation model such as ABCD was being used.

- **The community strengths assessment is not *per se* assessing levels of even community involvement in regeneration.** This requires a model that specifically focuses on involvement in a regeneration context whereas the strengths profile is primarily about assessing community capacity. A well-developed framework for assessing the level of involvement in regeneration areas is already available (COGS, 2000). Again, this work has informed the development of the community strengths profile and framework.

- **Community strengths profiles as described in this publication refer to neighbourhoods rather than communities of interest.** This is because the potential use of community strengths profiles with communities of interest has yet to be piloted. Unless otherwise stated, this handbook contains material that has been tried and tested. In principle, with appropriate and sensitive adaptation, community strengths profiles could be carried out with communities of interest and identity. This is looked at briefly in Part Five. The authors welcome development in this area.

There is further discussion on the role and scope of assessing community strengths in Part Five.

Community strengths assessments and the choice of areas for funding

Many cities and districts, through their local authorities and local strategic partnerships, are developing systematic approaches to the prioritisation of neighbourhoods for future allocation of resources available through major regeneration schemes. In this context, there is the possibility that community strengths profiles and the baseline information they provide could be used in a top-down way to influence the choice of area prioritised for the next available round of regeneration funding. The authors of this publication specifically request that community strengths assessments are not used in this way. The reasons for this are given in Part Six.

Terms used in this book

Community and voluntary groups – we use this phrase to mean both small-scale grass-roots community groups and voluntary organisations.

Support organisations – this includes any agency or organisation that provides support for community and voluntary groups. It may include the Council, the Health Authority, larger voluntary organisations, community resources centres and so on. For more information on the difference between community and voluntary groups, and support organisations, see Stage Two in Part Two, p. 24.

Support – we use this to mean practical, organisational and financial help for community and voluntary groups. This could be, for example, training, equipment, advice or funding. Part Three contains a comprehensive list of what this could mean in practice.

Assessing community strengths – this involves both carrying out the community strengths profile and applying the Community Strengths Framework.

Community strengths – this means community capacity but we prefer the term 'strengths' – and use it in this book – because it is more positive and less patronising!

Community capacity – the ability of local people, community groups and voluntary organisations to work together to take a leading and effective role in the development and regeneration of their communities and neighbourhoods.

Neighbourhood – we use this term interchangeably with the term 'area'.

Planning your
community strengths
profile

1 Planning your community strengths profile

A community strengths profile is a systematic description of an area that focuses on:

- **the level of community organisation** as indicated by the types of community and voluntary groups, their size, level of resources, skills, organisational structure and links with each other

- **the level of support** available to community groups and voluntary organisations active in the area, as indicated by the availability of advice, information, professional community work, training, practical resources and facilities.

Building such a profile involves assessing the state of health of the area's community and voluntary groups in as systematic a manner as possible. It also involves assessing the role of key projects, organisations and agencies that are providing support to groups in the area. Information for the profile can be collected through surveys, workshops and focus groups. Central to this approach is working closely with and involving local community groups in the process of assessing community strengths.

Finding out about the level of community organisation

The first main issue to identify in a community strengths profile is the overall level of community organisation in the area. This can be identified through a range of features:

☐ the general amount of community activity in the area, in terms of the range of community and voluntary groups

☐ the level of organisation of these groups, in terms of structure, membership, resources and funding

☐ the extent of community enterprise and initiatives by groups to generate income

☐ the level of skills and experience of the key members of these groups

☐ the capacity of groups to access training opportunities for their members

☐ the extent to which groups share skills and information and learn from each other

☐ the overall level of confidence, morale and optimism of the key members of groups

☐ the extent to which groups implement equal opportunities and challenge discrimination in their activities

☐ the extent of accountability of groups to their own members and neighbourhoods

☐ the extent and nature of links and good working relationships between groups for joint working and combined initiatives

☐ the extent of links and involvement of groups with agencies and the Council in joint planning of local services and new strategic initiatives

☐ the extent to which groups lead on projects and control assets in the community.

Some areas may already be well placed and well organised in all these features. Some may be at a lower level of organisation where community and voluntary groups are poorly organised and resourced, and work in an isolated manner making little use of funding opportunities or local networks. In general terms, this approach to profiling is based on the premise that areas which have voluntary and community groups that are already well-organised, reasonably resourced, linked to other local groups and have access to the information and training they need, can be seen as having greater strengths or 'capacity' than those that have low levels of organisation on any of these features.

Finding out about the level of support

The term 'support' here refers to a variety of ways in which larger organisations, projects and agencies help community and voluntary groups to be effective in achieving their aims. Support may be practical, such as use of rooms or equipment, or it may be organisational, such as help with funding and management issues. The level of available support in neighbourhoods can be identified through a range of features:

• the range of support organisations active in the area

• the level of advice, resources, funding and facilities provided by these support organisations

• the amount and type of training, and support for capacity building that is available

• the extent to which community capacity building is provided in a planned and co-ordinated manner based on identified needs

• the extent of help provided to groups in developing equal opportunities initiatives and tackling discrimination

• the extent to which support organisations themselves base their activities on equal opportunities

• the extent and nature of community work provision in the area

• the role and effectiveness of networks in the area

• the extent to which support organisations look at and respond to their own capacity building needs so that they work effectively with local communities.

Each of these features is explored in more detail with guidelines on how to obtain information regarding them (p. 21) and interpret the information gathered (p.46).

Level of Support

Resources, Facilities, Equipment, Space,
Advice, Funding, Training, Capacity building, Joint working,
Community work, Equal opportunities, Networks

Level of Community Organisation

Range, size and openness of local groups, Skills, confidence and
experience of group members, Resources, Equal opportunities,
Enterprise, Leadership, Joint working, Sharing skills,
Managing projects and assets

It should now be clear that a key aspect of this approach is that it involves assessing two different elements – the level of community organisation, and the level of support. It is these two elements in combination which can provide a broad-based picture of community strengths. This picture is obviously a simplified view of the world – but the division into two key elements helps to carry out an effective community strengths assessment. It is important to note that in community strengths profiles, support is not just seen as coming only from the larger organisations; within and between community groups there can also be a significant amount of support given and this is reflected in the features we listed in 'Level of community organisation', above.

Organising your community strengths profile

Community strengths profiles can be carried out by a variety of people such as:

- experienced members of community groups
- staff and volunteers from voluntary sector organisations
- practitioners or managers from projects, agencies or local authorities
- community workers
- youth workers.

This publication has been designed to enable the reader to understand and undertake, in liaison with other key groups and organisations, all the stages involved in the full version of a community strengths profile.

You will need particular resources and experience to undertake a community strengths profile, and these should be considered in advance. We discuss them below.

Parts Two and Three offer practical guidelines which are presented as a series of steps. Again in practice you may need to alter the order of the steps or adapt them to suit your own needs. They are presented in this way to highlight the issues involved in a clear and user-friendly manner rather than to suggest a set way of carrying out the surveys in every case. We include, too, checklists of survey questions as well as guidelines in the Resource sections on how to interpret the findings. These tried and tested questions for the surveys can be used as they are presented, or adapted to the needs of your area and the groups you may be working with.

Collecting the information

The type and amount of information to be collected from the two surveys – one on the level of community organisation and one on the level of support – may vary in each case depending on the area and on available resources. Careful consideration should also be given to the needs of different cultures to ensure that if your information gathering methods are organised in a way that is accessible to different parts of the community.

• Information can also be gathered through workshops and the use of focus groups. For each community profile the combination of methods used – survey, workshop and focus group – may vary depending on your needs and priorities.

• The key issue is that the information is collected systematically, using a variety of methods in order to check that information and findings gathered from one source has credibility and enough accuracy when checked out using a different method.

• Some of the information may already be available – it is important at an early stage to gather all available reports, surveys, directories and strategies that have any relation to community and voluntary groups in the area and the support work of larger organisations.

• The profile will need to combine both hard and soft data – that is, both quantitative and qualitative information. The information in a community strengths profile is gathered systematically and as objectively as possible, though the overall findings do not merely reflect hard data such as numbers of organisations providing training for community groups in the area. The quality of the support needs to be considered, not just that it is provided. Several questions in the survey questions checklist in Part Seven, Resources One and Two address this issue.

Once information is collected and analysed on both the level of organisation and the level of support, an action report can be drawn up that summarises the main findings. This can then be fed back at a workshop meeting and also to any key local networks or partnerships. Key conclusions from this process could then be used to inform decisions on new initiatives and the regeneration programme. The use of the profile's findings is discussed in Part Six.

What you will need to carry out a community strengths profile

There are five elements you will need to incorporate into your planning stage for carrying out a community strengths profile:

- local backing

- resources

- practical help with the survey of groups

- research skills

- overall co-ordination

Local backing

In order to carry out a community strengths profile you will need the backing of key community and voluntary groups in the area, as well as any key partnerships or networks. It is recommended that without this backing you do not proceed with the strengths profile. This issue is discussed more in Part Two. In some cases, it may be that local groups themselves through their own network or partnership will lead on organising and carrying out the whole community strengths profile.

Resources

The full version of the community strengths profile involves two surveys, at least one open workshop, and possibly several focus group meetings. So you will need the resources of time and money to organise these, including administrative support, as well as to prepare an action-oriented report based on the findings. The size of the surveys – and thus the costs – will vary depending on the size of the area and how much the surveys are carried out through personal visits or postal questionnaire. This is discussed in Part Two.

Practical help with the survey of groups

For some of this work, you will need the assistance of one or two people who know the area and have some experience of working with community groups. For the community groups survey, it is recommended that personal visits are made to groups rather than just using a postal survey. Consequently, this will require people with good communication skills who have some experience of community and voluntary groups. This may be locally-based community workers, experienced residents who can act as community researchers or, possibly with the appropriate background, commercial researchers. Whatever the source, the people providing this practical help will need to be briefed fully so that they can assist and support individual representatives from community and voluntary groups when they are completing the questionnaire. For a survey of 30 groups, for example, this will take approximately 60 hours.

Research skills

You will also need the assistance of someone with research skills. This will be partly to help you to design the layout of your questionnaire form. In addition, entering the information gathered into a computer-based programme and then providing an initial analysis may require approximately three days of their time. Some of the actual data entry could be carried out by an administrator, which may reduce the time needed for the researcher. However, unless a manual system is used, this type of technical support will be vital to access and analyse the information collected from the surveys.

Overall co-ordination

All these different elements require overall co-ordination. The person taking the lead role in organising the community strengths profile will need to have had some prior experience of working with communities and be able to use this experience in an objective manner. This person may, for example, be a regeneration partnership manager, a council officer, a community worker, a member of a community group, a development worker from a local agency or a consultant. The co-ordination role does not depend on the lead person themselves having research skills or experience – though some support in this area is recommended. The key point, however, is that whatever organisation they are from, they should personally have some experience of working with community and voluntary groups and have a commitment to adopting a community development approach.

Surveying the level of community organisation 2

2 Surveying the level of community organisation

We now move on to describe how to carry out the practical work involved in producing a community strengths profile. This is dealt with in three different sections, Parts Two, Three and Four. This Part looks at how to set up and organise a survey of community and voluntary groups in the area, which combined with other information, can be used to assess the level of community organisation. This survey of community and voluntary activity forms the heart of the community strengths profile.

Introduction to the survey

The work involved in the survey is broken down into six main stages. The stages are briefly introduced then each stage is looked at in more detail:

- *Stage One*
  Initial meetings and discussion with key community and voluntary groups as well as support organisations active in the area. The main aim of this is to discuss, and hopefully get approval for the idea of carrying out a profile. There is also the need to agree on the area to be covered and begin to develop some local ownership of the work of the profile.

- *Stage Two*
  This involves obtaining information to build up a comprehensive, up-to-date list of community groups and voluntary organisations active in the area.

- *Stage Three*
  Decide how you will carry out the survey and select the sample of groups.

- *Stage Four*
  Choose the range of questions to be included in your community groups questionnaire.

- *Stage Five*
  Gather the information needed either through personal visits or through postal survey.

- *Stage Six*
  Analyse the information gathered. This involves collating the completed forms and, if using a database, entering the data. It involves drawing out initial key findings.

At a later point you will need to combine the findings from the survey of community and voluntary organisations with the findings from the survey of support organisations (see Part Four, below).

In planning your work on the seven stages or steps you will need to:

- consider what changes you might need to make to the order of these proposed stages to respond to local needs of your area. The stages are described in a concrete way in order to describe clearly the practical work involved – this is intended as an aid to understanding, not as a set formula for carrying out the work

- begin to plan the survey of the level of support at the same time as carrying out the survey on the level of community organisation. See Part Three for further details.

It is important to note that carrying out the level of community organisation survey will take approximately three to four months from the first consultation meetings to when the final report is actually available.

We now move on to look in more detail at the planning and practical work involved.

Stage One

The main purposes of Stage One are to clarify the aims of the profile, to obtain local backing for carrying it out, and to agree on the area to be covered by the profile. It also includes involving local groups in the work of the community profile itself.

Clarifying the aims and obtaining local backing

As we described in Part One, a community strengths profile can be used in a variety of ways. It will be crucial at an early stage to be clear on which roles your community strengths profile is intended to cover. In order to do this, it will be worth contacting key groups and organisations in the area, ideally through a broad-based network or community partnership. The range of potential roles can be discussed and agreed on, and the aims written down as an aid to effective planning. In terms of obtaining local backing, if the area already has a regeneration programme, it may be important to contact the board of directors of the regeneration partnership and obtain approval for the community profile to be carried out. It is also worth consulting or informing the following that the survey is about to happen:

- key local leaders and community activists
- local Members of the Council
- key agencies and projects active in the area
- community workers and youth workers.

In obtaining support for the profile, the following issues will need to be clarified:

☐ What are the costs and resources involved and who will cover them?

☐ In whose name will the survey be carried out?

☐ Who will own and have access to the information gathered?

☐ What arrangements will be made for confidentiality and data protection?

☐ Will the information gathered be used to produce a local directory of groups?

☐ What research has been carried out in the area already? How can this be built on and used?

☐ What use will be made of the final report?

☐ Will it be used to inform decision-making in the area and by whom?

This clarity of intended use is especially important if the material being collected will be used to produce a local directory. Groups completing the survey will need to know in advance if some of the information will be made public. The survey forms will thus need a covering letter to say who is carrying out the profile and why. Consequently these issues need to be sorted out early on with broad agreement on how the information will be used.

If there have been other community surveys recently in the area, it will be important to make it clear why the community profile is being carried out and what new information it will produce.

Agreeing on the area

The area may be easily definable either because there are already clear, well-known boundaries, such as rivers or major roads, or because it may already have been identified in some way for regeneration initiatives. If this is the case, it will simply be a matter of confirming that this is the area that the profile will cover. If not, the area will need to be agreed on in advance of Stage Two. Bear in mind:

- a ward or administrative boundary may not have any meaning to local people

- it may be more useful to use boundaries that local people themselves use and relate to, such as a main road

- also look at regeneration plans in neighbouring areas because these may include boundaries.

Two key points to consider when choosing the area to be profiled are:

- the size of the area you profile may have a major impact on the effectiveness of the survey (this is discussed in Stage Three)

- even with a clearly defined boundary, in practice it is useful for the survey to include some groups and centres slightly outside this boundary. This reflects the fact that people will obviously make use of neighbouring facilities and resources. We recommend if a centre is located outside the boundary but is used regularly by people who live within the target area and is walking distance away, then it should be included in the survey. This reflects the fact that the resources used by a community do not keep within a tightly defined perimeter line. By using walking distance, rather than driving distance, as the criteria, it limits the extent of this in a realistic manner.

Involving groups in the work of the profile

Locally-based community and voluntary groups in the area can be involved in the work of the survey itself. This could involve a number of options:

- forming a steering group to guide the work of the profile
- involving people in practical help with information gathering
- involving groups in the workshop.

The minimum form of involvement in the process is that groups will be invited at a later stage to the workshop where the findings are presented and discussed. Forming a local steering group for the profile is very useful as a source of information when building up the full list of local groups. As long as this group is broadly representative, it should help to increase the response rate to the survey, especially as it is a way of building up trust and interest in the profile.

Using local people on a paid basis as community researchers means that some residents will have an opportunity to get more involved. This may involve organising training sessions in interview skills and techniques. There are likely to be additional administrative tasks to sort out payment and expenses. Overall there are both advantages and disadvantages to employing local people. For example, they may provide a point of entry to 'hard to reach' groups, but some groups may also be less open in their responses if they already know the interviewer. If local people are employed on a paid basis to carry out the survey, it is important that the recruitment for the work is open to anyone interested and the work is advertised locally. However, in temporary work such as this care needs to be taken not to interfere with people's welfare benefits entitlements either through the amount of hours they are working or the payment they receive. Consequently the benefits of working with local interviewers need to be balanced against these additional demands in planning the way the survey is carried out.

Involving local people – the experience from Bradford

The pilot of the community organisations survey in Allerton and Lower Grange in Bradford involved three local residents as community researchers to carry out the interviews with community groups. This included some informal training on how to use the questionnaire form, as well as payment for the time involved. Using local residents added a lot to the survey – they already knew many of the groups in the area which helped them in drawing up a comprehensive list.

Stage Two

This involves building up a comprehensive, up-to-date list of community groups and voluntary organisations active in the area. The sources for this information could include:

- local libraries
- agencies and key local projects

- existing directories

- locally based community and youth workers

- community groups themselves

- schools and religious centres

- council officers who know the area well

- organisations that fund local groups

- district-wide voluntary sector support organisations such as a Council for Voluntary Service

- the local media.

Here are some examples of types of community groups and voluntary organisations that could be included on your list:

residents' associations	tenants' associations
community centres	family centres
community based projects	playgroups
community enterprises	development trusts
youth groups	women's groups
disability groups	pensioners' clubs
advice centres	drug projects
social clubs	activity groups
environmental action	allotments committees
and campaigning groups	self-help support groups
neighbourhood watch groups	churches, mosques and temples
religious groups	cultural groups
festival committees	working men's clubs.
sports groups	

At this stage in the profile all that is needed is the name of the group, a contact name, address and telephone number and an idea of the type of people who make up the group's users or members. The latter may be needed in choosing groups for the sample as described on p. 27. In collecting such information, you will need to consider the following issues:

- This list is of community groups and voluntary organisations. For the survey of level of community organisation, it does not need to and should not include council departments, agencies, schools, leisure centres, shops, pubs, health centres, housing associations, private companies, regeneration partnerships, and large public organisations. Some of the latter may be included in the level of support survey. This list does not include voluntary organisations and community projects whose main purpose is to support other community and voluntary groups. These would definitely be included in the level of support survey. The list does not include networks – these are a special case and information on these can be collected by asking groups and organisations that belong to them.

- Compiling this list of community groups and voluntary organisations will take some time and effort. The aim at this stage is to include every community group and voluntary organisation in the area. This is so that in selecting those that will be surveyed, the sample is representative of the total.

- Bear in mind that when building this list of groups, the response you will often get at first is 'there are not many groups around here' and 'we know them all already so there's no need to ask any further'. There really is a need to be systematic in building up a full list of groups in the area, especially small ones which may not be included in existing databases, or known only in certain circles. It is important that effort is put into this stage, otherwise only the larger, already known groups will be included in the profile, thus excluding the grass-roots, smaller groups.

- Cultural factors may be an issue here in that certain groups are only known in certain networks and neighbourhoods. Sensitivity is needed to build links with different parts of the community and ensure the list includes groups associated with different cultures and identities in the area.

- There may be some groups that are hidden behind another purpose. For example, the local Oxfam or Age Concern charity shop may well be run by a local group or have a community group attached to it. Equally a school may have a community group meeting in its building. You will need to decide whether such groups are 'in' or 'out' of the survey.

An issue that needs resolving is when several groups are based in one building or community centre. Does the centre management committee or co-ordinator complete one form on behalf of the different user groups or should each group receive its own form? The latter may mean unnecessary duplication, especially if the groups are quite small. However, if a user group could potentially be based in a different building and is only in effect renting space in the centre, then that group should have its own questionnaire. In addition, groups that are of a very temporary nature or where there is not an on-going group, such as an evening class, are not worth including in the survey.

As discussed, some groups will need to be included on the list even though not located directly in the target area. This is acceptable when people who live in the target area use or belong to such groups or centres. Local knowledge can be used in drawing up the list of how many such neighbouring groups and centres need to be included. As described on p. 23, the criteria need to be based on reasonable walking distance from the boundary of the target area.

Stage Three

Stage Three involves deciding how you will actually carry out the survey and which questions you will include on the survey form from the full range of questions provided in Resource One.

The ideal solution would be to visit and interview representatives of all known groups! In some cases, depending on the size of the area and the amount of help available, this will in fact be possible. The recommended method of information collection for the community organisation survey is through personal visits. These would be arranged with one or two representatives of each group, completing the form through an informal interview held usually in the group's own building or meeting place.

Actually completing the form during each visit will take an average of two hours for one person to carry out, when travel, and time for introductions, are included. You will consequently need to estimate how many groups could be visited given the amount of help available. Note that as suggested on p. 17, the work of carrying out this survey requires either an experienced community worker or community researchers who have been provided with some training.

If however, with the hours of help available, not all groups can be visited for an informal interview, you could combine a postal survey with interviews through personal visits so that all known groups still see the questionnaire form and have the opportunity to respond. Telephone contact to complete the questionnaire form is another alternative, which combines an element of a personal approach but eliminates the travel time.

Choosing the survey method

The benefits and disadvantages of visits, and a postal survey, need to be compared and considered. Visits have the following main advantages:

- Through a personal visit, less resourced or less confident groups can be encouraged to complete the form. From a social inclusion perspective, ensuring there is some outreach work to involve marginalised groups is an important consideration.

- The response rate will generally be significantly higher than with a postal survey.

- If needed, more complex questions can be added to the questionnaire which the interviewer can explain, such as ranking of possible preferences.

- Through visits, new links and contacts can be built up with groups.

- Personal contact can enhance the opportunity for reflection and developmental thinking as the questionnaire is worked through.

- The likelihood of ambiguity in answering the questions is reduced.

Against this there are some disadvantages:

- The person carrying out the visits may influence how the form is completed.

- Visits involve vastly more time than a postal survey. In other words, the number of groups receiving the questionnaire form can be increased through use of the postal survey method.

If the two methods are to be combined, one option is to use the visits specifically for smaller, less confident groups. The larger voluntary organisations with paid staff are more likely to complete the form on their own. One way of increasing the number of groups that receive a personal visit is to use the visit just to introduce the survey and explain how to complete the form, leaving the group member to fill it in later and then return it in a stamped addressed envelope. This saves time for each visit but still offers some contact and support. The response rate – the proportion of completed forms returned compared to the total posted or left during visits – can be increased by friendly follow-up letters or phone calls once the deadline date for their return has been reached.

We recommend that all the community and voluntary groups identified in your full list of local groups are included in the survey. If this creates too large a number of groups to be surveyed, whatever combination of methods you use, it may be that the area you have chosen is too large.

> ### Planning your survey – the experience from Horton Grange, Bradford
>
> Some areas may need additional community worker time to help to make contact and involve groups in the survey. The community profile pilot in Horton Grange, Bradford, produced useful points about this process. The area is a lively inner city part of Bradford with many isolated groups as well as an important new local partnership and some innovative centres. The experience in this area showed that where groups are isolated, additional time may be needed for outreach.

Stage Four

Design your questionnaire

A checklist of questions is provided in Part Seven, Resource One below. It has been designed only as a checklist or menu to choose from, and is too long to used fully as it stands. Please note it is not a ready-made questionnaire form! It is worth reading through the checklist of questions and getting a clear idea of what each question is trying to find out. In adapting it to your needs, there are a number of points to consider:

☐ **You may want to add new questions to reflect the issues that groups are facing in your area**
This will make the survey more in touch with the area. Equally there may be some questions that are not appropriate for your area, or which you decide would be better covered in a workshop or focus group meeting.

☐ **Be aware of the time implications of open-ended questions**
Compared to questions that only provide a limited range of options with a set of boxes to tick against, the responses from open-ended questions are more time consuming to analyse. However, they will often produce even insights that are very useful for the profile. A balance between these factors will need to be achieved in planning what combination of question *you* choose from the checklist.

☐ **Ensure some questions address issues of quality**
Some assessment of quality is a key part of the profile method. Several of the questions included in the checklist look at issues of the perceived quality of the support provided, not just the amount, by asking about level of satisfaction. It is advisable to keep these included in your questionnaire. You may wish to add more

questions that ask about the level of satisfaction of support received in order to further look at this issue.

☐ **You may need to add codes to your questions**
Where questions involve several options to choose from, it is useful in advance to give each option a number. This can be in very small print so it does not distract from the main question numbering. It does help when entering data at a later stage. The same can be done with open-ended questions – for such details we recommend you get advice from a researcher.

☐ **Pilot your tailor-made questionnaire**
Try it out on colleagues and, with their support, several groups or organisations that are representative of the larger survey list. This will be crucial to ensure the questionnaire has a clear layout, is meaningful, is not too long and will produce the information you require.

☐ **You may be producing a directory as part of the outcome of the survey**
The checklist of questions in Part Seven, Resource One below can also be used to draw up a set of questions specifically for a directory. Obviously other new additional questions may need to be added depending on the role of your directory. It is important when collecting information that the person completing the form is fully aware that some of the information will be used in this way. This needs to be made clear to groups, otherwise it can cause problems later when information is made publicly available, to which they did not agree. These questions can be marked in a particular way in the questionnaire or even grouped together into a separate introductory section.

General points on producing community directories

Agree on aims
Before you decide what information to collect it is worth being clear on what the aims of the directory are. This will influence the range of questions you include in the questionnaire. For example is the directory for the main benefit of individuals or for community groups?

Agree on format
Format means the way in which the information will be distributed – booklet, leaflet, poster, ring binder or website. A website may be cheap to set up and relatively easy to update compared to a printed version. However if a website is the only form of dissemination, it may exclude groups who can not or do not want to use computer-based communication.

Level of detail
For directories it is generally not worth including very detailed information concerning activities eg the play group meets on Wednesdays at 9.30 am. This level of detail goes out of date very quickly.

Consider equality issues
Some information may be crucial for minorities to be able to use the directory. For example information on access into and within buildings.

Consider additional information
As well as the information collected on groups, you may want to add extra information. This could include a general introduction to the area, a list of key service providers, useful contacts etc.

Proof read with care
Since the information is to be reproduced in some form, it is worth checking the final typed text against the original on the completed forms. In particular check the telephone number, it is the single most important thing to get right!

Stage Five

Organise the information gathering

In carrying out the survey there are a number of practical points to consider and plan for. These will vary depending on the extent to which your survey is postal or visit-based.

Visits

If your survey is to be carried out through visits, it is essential to send a covering letter in advance of contacting the groups. When you phone a group to arrange a visit they will then have some idea of who you are. The covering letter needs to state who is carrying out the survey, with what local backing, why and how the information will be used for example, a directory or action report. It should also say who needs to be available for the visit and for how long. The people carrying out the visits will need some form of identification – identity badges are useful.

You will also need to be very clear about the level of confidentiality of the information being collected. Some people may be concerned that their group will be individually named in a report. Consequently, it is important to be clear on how the information will be used. Here is an example from the Bradford New Deal for Communities survey; this information was provided to groups before they completed the survey form:

Bradford New Deal for Communities Survey

How the information will be used

'The aim of this survey is to build up a picture of the needs and resources of community and voluntary groups. This can be used to help to plan new initiatives in the area. Once the survey has been completed, draft findings will be drawn up with key points for the way forward. There will be an open workshop in October when the draft findings are discussed. A report will then be written based on this and sent out to all groups in the area and the New Deal for Communities partnership board.

Please note that this report will contain a summary of the information collected but not give detailed information about particular groups.'

- If a community worker or community researchers are carrying out the survey through visits, ensure that they have received any induction training and background information needed. They are likely to know some of the groups already, so it will be important that they do not distort the information collected through a pre-set view of the group. The induction training will also need to include an introduction to the questionnaire and the purpose of each question. See Part Four, pp. 46–54 below for additional background information on particular questions that will assist you in doing this.

- They may also need some guidance on interview techniques so that answers are not influenced unduly by the person carrying out the survey.

- Some visits can have the role of introducing the questionnaire form rather than completing it with the group representative at that time. Leaving it with them to complete later can save a lot of the time for the interviewer, while still providing a back-up phone number and perhaps a stamped addressed envelope. Another possibility is after the first visit, the interviewer arranges to drop by in a few days' time to collect the completed form.

- In visiting groups you may find out about other groups not already on your list. You will need to consider if these should be included in your sample.

Postal

If your survey is based totally or partly on sending the questionnaires out through the post, you will need to organise the following:

- Send out the questionnaire form with a covering letter with similar information on who is carrying it out, etc as described above. Wherever possible, address it to a named individual, not just 'sir/madam/colleague'.

- Give at least a four-week period, with a deadline date, for the return of the completed forms. Providing an addressed envelope increases the response rate but including a stamp on it can not usually be justified in terms of further increased response.

- Once this deadline is nearly up, telephone those groups that have not returned it with a friendly reminder. Experience has shown that this type of follow-up phone call increases the response rate by a significant degree. It could also be an opportunity to complete the form over the phone.

- These follow-up phone calls can also identify groups that may be struggling with completing the form and need a visit to help them through it. This is especially important if there is a pattern emerging of the rate of response of some types of groups being below that of other groups.

- At a certain point, despite reminders and friendly follow-up phone calls, there will be a cut-off point where further effort is unlikely to reap further completed forms and may actually alienate people!

In terms of planning, the survey will take between four and eight weeks to carry out, whether postal or through visits. A surgery session could be held during this period to provide help for any groups not finding it easy to fill the form in. At the end of the period, a stocktake needs to be carried out on the returned forms to ensure you have achieved a desired number and range of groups. If not, further outreach work may be needed to ensure you achieve a valid sample of groups to work with.

Issues to consider in carrying out the survey

☐ **Which group member completes the form?**
The response you get from a staff member may be different from the Chairperson of the group. Where possible it is best in arranging visits to meet two people from each group in order to cater for this and/or to ensure that they represent the management committee of the group, where there is one, rather than mainly representing the staff's interests and concerns. Where there is a divergence of views this can be noted with their approval on the final section of the form.

☐ **What information is not needed?**
Some larger voluntary groups that work outside the target area may complete the form with information on their activities across the whole district. It is important that only their activity in the target area is the subject of the profile because information relating to a much wider area will distort the figures. The checklist questions in Part Seven, Resource One below have been designed with this point in mind but even so, explanation and reminders are useful.

☐ **Will the answers to the questions be truthful?**
Some distortion may occur because leaders in groups may not want to reveal problems the group is facing – and in some cases they may be the problem! Another possibility is that groups want to present themselves as well organised in order to gain a good reputation for future funding opportunities. To some extent these issues can be catered for by using other methods of gathering information through the workshops and focus group meetings. These are designed to act as a safety net to check on this issue but not to invite comments on any one group's condition.

☐ **What if a group sees itself as both a group and a support organisation?**
In such cases it is crucial to work with them to make a decision on which is their most dominant role and only complete one form not two. Completing two forms, one from each category will complicate the figures produced.

Stage Six

Analysing the information

Information from the completed questionnaires will then need to be combined to produce a broad picture of the community groups and voluntary organisations in the area. We now move on to the process of analysing the information collected from the completed questionnaire forms.

- The very first action at this point is to number all forms and then photocopy all forms. This is a basic security measure to avoid loss as they are moved between desks or even buildings.

- The answers given to open-ended questions can be compared to identify any common issues. The responses to each open-ended question can then be categorised on this basis.

- Broadly, the aim of the analysis is to identify frequencies. For example how many groups do not have a constitution? How many regard funding as a significant problem and so on.

- A development of this is to break it down further into categories. For example, it may be useful to know if it is a particular type of group that has funding as a major problem. This is called cross-tabulation or cross-referencing. We strongly suggest that unless you already have skills in this area, at this point you get help from someone with research skills.

There are now at least two further key questions to consider.

How will you categorise the responses?

It may be useful to divide the groups broadly into community sector and voluntary sector. This is because research has shown that smaller grass-roots groups often have quite different needs from larger ones, which may include branches of nationally based charities. Also some voluntary organisations may, for example, have quite large levels of income, and combined figures of voluntary and community sector would distort the local picture of how grass-roots groups are doing. A simple basis for this division is to use the number of staff employed by the organisation.

The Bradford New Deal for Communities data showed that out of 32 voluntary and community groups who returned the completed forms, 25 came into the category of having four or less full-time staff or equivalent. The groups with four full-time staff or over were called 'larger voluntary organisations' and their data was analysed separately. In this case using the definition based on up to four full-time staff or equivalent produced some useful findings. It showed a difference in level of organisation between the two categories. It is worth noting that there is no nationally accepted definition of the difference between community and voluntary sector but a variety of approaches abound (see Chanan, Garratt and West, 2000). So it may be helpful in some cases to use, for example, a lower number of staff than four as the dividing line. According to research by NCVO (Passey et al., 2000) in the late 1990s, at least three-quarters of all community and voluntary organisations across the country have no paid staff at all. It is likely that this would also be true of most localities, so any survey in which half or more of the groups identified do have even a single paid staff member is likely to be overlooking considerable numbers of small, low-profile groups.

More ideas on how to categorise the data are given in Part Four, p. 46, below.

What system will you use to analyse the data?

For analysing the 'hard data' that is the information given in response to questions which are quantifiable, there are three main options:

(a) Book a room for a day and use flip charts to write up and manually add up figures to identify trends. The totals can be added up out of the total sample. For example, out of 30 groups surveyed it may show 20 have no constitution, 25 have had no training over the last year, none have received outside advice, and 15 have an income per year of below £1,000.

(b) Use a spreadsheet such as Excel to enter the data and compile numbers. Some text can be entered into most spreadsheets. Statistical information can be converted into graphs, tables and charts which may be useful for presentation of the information.

(c) Use a statistical software package such as the Statistical Programme for Social Sciences (SPSS). This will involve coding and entering the data as well as an initial analysis.

Option (a), while old fashioned, does have the advantage of being more participatory, if this is appropriate. It is, however, time-consuming with a large sample of groups, and suffers a lack of ability to easily produce cross-referencing between different questions. SPSS nowadays is relatively accessible if you have the support of a researcher experienced in its use, and is a powerful tool for producing cross-tabulations. Generally speaking, the larger the sample and the larger the number of questions, the stronger the case is for using a statistical package. The main limitation of SPSS is that it does not easily convert data into even visually interesting formats such as pie charts.

As well as the hard data, the questionnaire form in Part Seven, Resource One, below, includes questions which are not easily translated into figures. It is important that this information is also collated and used as part of the profile. This will involve carefully reading through all forms and, for each such question, identifying any common themes. Broad categories can be developed based on these, and the responses to each question identified where they match these. Further numerical data can thus be extracted from the raw soft data.

As you can see, the process of analysing the information gathered takes time, and this time will need to be built into the plan of how the community profile is carried out. Having collected lots of information, it is important to use it – rather than file it away or put it on a shelf to collect dust. There is nothing more demoralising for participating groups and organisations than to be asked for information but not to receive any follow-up afterwards.

The Bradford New Deal for Communities Survey

A survey of 25 community and voluntary groups showed:

- nearly half of all these groups have 9 or less active members
- nearly half of the groups (48%) have 20 or less users per week
- 18 groups have a management committee, 6 do not
- 5 groups have no constitution, 13 do, 1 is a limited company, and 10 are registered charities
- overall the majority of groups are run by their own members (16 out of 25 groups) but 8 groups are dependent on one key individual in the group to keep it going.

Surveying the level of support

3 Surveying the level of support

This section describes the second key part of the practical work involved in producing a community strengths profile. Part Two looked at how to set up and organise a survey of community and voluntary groups in the area, which combined with other information, can be used to assess the level of community organisation. Part Three examines how to survey the organisations in the area that provide support to these community and voluntary groups, in order to identify the level of support.

Again, the way to collect this type of information is described as a series of steps or stages which can be then adapted to the particular needs and problems of your area. Alternatively, some of this information could be collected through open meetings or focus groups. The steps given here describe using a survey as the main method.

Stage One: Consulting key organisations

Much of this consultation will have been carried out as a part of the preparatory work in the survey of community and voluntary groups. This is especially the case if the two surveys are to run parallel to each other. In particular it is important to ensure that key providers of support feel they know what is happening and will be open to looking at the survey's findings once available.

Stage Two: Building up a list of organisations

A key step is to identify all the organisations in the area that may be providing support to community groups and voluntary organisations. In order to do this we need to be clear as to what 'support' means! Support may take the form of practical help, training, advice, funding, facilities, resources, equipment, information or staff time. The following types of organisations may be providing support:

larger voluntary organisations

the health authority and health action zones

community projects

religious centres and organisations

regeneration partnerships

the council

the council for voluntary service

community and resources centres

local businesses

Any one organisation may only be providing a limited range of support from the full checklist available. In this publication, such organisations, where they are providing any such support as listed below are called 'support organisations'.

In practice drawing up the list of support organisations will be reasonably easy. Use can be made of community workers, groups, networks, agencies, ward members and local leaders for addresses and contacts, as well as any existing lists held by the Council or agencies.

Key issues to consider

☐ **Does the list just contain organisations that are based in the area or ones that are based outside it but are active in the area?**
In practice it is more effective to include both, even though some of the latter may be district-wide organisations, otherwise a large section of available support will be ignored. The key issue to note, however, is that the checklist of questions in Part Seven, Resource Two, below, is explicit in asking these organisations about their work in the target area, not the pattern of what they do district-wide. The sample questions are designed on this basis and any adaptations need to bear this in mind.

☐ **Is 'support' the best word to use?**
As long as 'support' is given a clear meaning then yes, it does seem to be the most effective term to use. Terms such as 'capacity building' need much more explaining and some organisations may wrongly assume they are not appropriate. Whatever the term used, the crucial issue is to be explicit that this concerns support for community and voluntary groups, not for individuals. The whole approach of this community profile is that it is based on the needs and strengths of community and voluntary groups – this refers to existing groupings of people with some form of on-going organisation, not just a term referring to a social category, such as 'the unemployed'. Many agencies and organisations, especially those that do not necessarily have much experience of community development, will automatically think the term 'community group' can be used in this looser way.

What do we mean by 'support'?

We provide here some examples of support often provided by projects, agencies, larger voluntary sector organisations and local authorities for community and voluntary groups.

Support that helps to build community organisations
Grant aid; access to rooms and halls for meetings; access to office space and equipment; free or cheap office furniture; practical assistance with administration; access to low-cost auditors; access to funding information. Access to computers with word processing, spreadsheet, database and desktop publishing programs; access to the Internet, laser printers; printing equipment; photocopier; fax and franking machines; presentation materials and display boards; overhead projectors, flip chart paper and video equipment. Advice on team work and business planning; information on funding sources and making bids; legal information; professional advice from architects and auditors; information on constitutions and financial planning, guidance on partnerships and legal structures; advice on employing staff; secretarial assistance.

Support that helps to build involvement
Employing staff who help new community groups to get established and develop their structures and organisation, and who can provide practical support and administration for groups and networks; providing help for groups to find out about local needs and work jointly with other groups and agencies; involving community groups in contributing to local decision making, having a real say and influence over local issues.

Support that helps to build skills, knowledge and confidence
Organise or directly provide training courses designed for members of voluntary and community groups; books and videos on managing projects; grants and childcare to help people involved in groups' access training courses; information on how the Council works; mentoring schemes for members of community groups; practical help with groups to organise visits to other centres and projects as a learning opportunity; resource library on capacity building and community development.

Support that helps to build equality
Providing training on cultural awareness for community groups; help with writing equal opportunities policies and action plans, running campaigns; Information on equal opportunities issues and relevant legislation.
    Providing guidelines on recruitment and selection procedures; access to translators and signers; grant aid to make buildings accessible; provision of equipment such as portable hearing loops; access to Braille production; space, staff and equipment for crèches for meetings, events and courses.

Stage Three: Decisions about your survey

Stage Three involves making two main decisions:

- decide on which organisations from the full list will be selected for the actual survey

- decide on how you will collect the information, whether by interview or postal survey.

In practice there will usually be less support organisations in an area than community and voluntary groups. The Bradford pilot, for example, identified 48 community and voluntary groups in the New Deal for Communities area, and surveyed 22 support organisations. In addition, support organisations, which will usually be staffed organisations, are more likely to be able to respond to a postal questionnaire than grass-roots community and voluntary groups. This raises two points:

- it is worth including all identified support organisations in your survey

- using just a postal method of information collection can still produce a reasonable number of returned completed forms, especially if reminders are sent and word of mouth encouragement given through meetings and phone calls.

There are still, however, time permitting, some distinct advantages to additional use of personal visits for interviews where possible. Often this can add more depth to the answers given to the questions as well as promote a sense of ownership in the whole profile's aims.

Stage Four: Design your questionnaire

Part Seven, Resource Two includes a checklist of questions you can use in planning your questionnaire. In adapting it to your needs, there are two points to consider:

☐ **You may want to add new questions to reflect the issues that organisations are facing in your area**.
Equally there may be some questions that are not appropriate for your area. Consequently it is worth reading through the questionnaire and getting a clear idea of what each question is trying to find out. Again it is useful to carry out a short pilot with your questionnaire to check that it will produce the information you require.

☐ **You may be producing a directory as part of the outcome of the survey**.
If so, other new additional questions may need to be added depending on the role of your directory. It is important when collecting information that will be printed in a local directory that the person completing the form is fully aware that the information in that part of the form will be used in this way. This needs to be made clear to organisations otherwise it can cause problems later when information is made publicly available that they did not agree to. These questions can be marked in a particular way in the questionnaire or even grouped together into a separate section. Included in Part Two, pp. 29–30 are some basic points on how to produce community directories.

Issues to consider in carrying out the survey

☐ **What information is not needed?**
Some support organisations that also work outside the target area may complete the form with information on their activities across the whole city/district. It is important that only their activity in the target area is the subject of the profile because information given relating to a much wider area will distort the figures. The questions on the form have been designed with this point in mind, but even so explanation and reminders are useful.

☐ **What if a group sees themselves as both a group and a support organisation?**
In such cases it is crucial to work with them to make a decision on which is their most dominant role and only complete one survey form, not two. Completing two survey forms, one from each category, will complicate the figures produced which will not then add up to the total samples.

Stage Five: Collecting and collating the completed forms

Information from the completed questionnaires will then need to be combined to produce a broad picture of the support organisations active in the area. Some key tasks are:

• The very first action point is to number all forms and then photocopy them. This is a basic security measure to avoid loss as they are moved between desks or even buildings

- The answers given to open-ended questions can be compared to identify any common issues. The responses to each open-ended question can then be categorised on this basis

- The responses to all questions will need to be entered into an appropriate software programme if using a computer-based form of analysis.

For the remaining work on collating and analysing the information gathered, please refer to the process outlined for the survey of community groups in Part Two, pp. 33–34 it is broadly similar to the process you need to go through with the data from the survey of support organisations.

If you have followed the stages described so far in Parts Two and Three, you will by now have the data collected and analysed. This will produce what are called frequencies: for example, 25% of groups do not have a constitution; 50% of support organisations offer training to community groups. But what does it all mean? The figures on their own do not necessarily say much and need interpreting. We now move on to look at how to interpret the initial findings.

*Interpreting the
findings* •4

4 Interpreting the findings

In this Part we provide guidelines on interpreting the information gathered from the two surveys. This will produce a set of draft findings and draft conclusions that can be discussed in the workshop. We begin by introducing four key themes that can be used to divide the information collected from the two surveys. We then provide a detailed commentary on the questions from both surveys so that you will be able to draw out key points from the available hard and soft data. In order to bring this to life, we use the surveys carried out in the Bradford New Deal for Communities area as a major case study.

Introducing the four themes

The next step in the work of carrying out the community strengths assessment is to make some sense of the information gathered in the two surveys. This can lead to a set of draft findings that can be presented for discussion at the Workshop – ideas on how to do this are given in Part Five. The aim here in Part Four is to look at the majority of the questions provided in Part Seven, Resources One and Two, and give an outline of how to interpret the information you have gathered. This will involve handling a large amount of information, and to make this easier, it is helpful to divide the questions up into categories. You will find that the questions in both survey checklists in Resources One and Two are divided into four such categories or themes. These four themes are used to assist in understanding the information gathered and can be used for the presentation for the Workshop. The four themes are:

- building organisations
- building skills
- building equality
- building involvement.

Building organisations

This is about the development of community and voluntary groups, and how they may work with other groups. It concerns, too, the ways in which community and small voluntary groups are supported to develop their strength and organisational capacity.

It is also about the effectiveness of networks and support organisations in supporting community and voluntary groups.

Building skills

This is about the ways in which groups build the skills, knowledge and confidence of their members to enable them to be effective in achieving their aims and to fully participate in, and benefit from, regeneration and community development. It is also about the skills and abilities of people working and involved in local partnerships and support organisations.

Building equality

Building equality is about the ways in which community and voluntary groups are inclusive, and the extent to which they try to help to build equality within their group and in communities. It is also about the ways support organisations themselves contribute to these initiatives.

Building involvement

This is about the extent to which community and voluntary groups involve people, and contribute to and influence local decision-making. It also concerns the ways support organisations help to build the capacity of community and voluntary groups to be able to do this.

These four themes are based on a widely used evaluation model of community development called 'ABCD, Achieving Better Community Development' (Barr and Hashagen, 2000a, b and c). The terms used for the four themes in assessing community strengths have been changed slightly from ABCD in order to simplify their use in this context. The ABCD model has been consciously used for the community strengths profile assessment in order to ensure linkage between the two approaches, and make use of current work in community development theory.

The community groups survey questions

To make use of the four themes, we first need to take a look at the level of community organisation. As described in Part One, the features concerning the level of community organisation that can be examined are the:

- general amount of community activity in the area in terms of the range of community and voluntary groups

- level of organisation of these groups in terms of structure, membership, resources and funding

- extent of community enterprise and initiatives by groups to generate income

- level of skills and experience of the key members of these groups

- capacity of groups to access training opportunities for all their members

- extent to which groups share practice and learn from each other

- overall level of confidence, morale and optimism of the key members of groups

- extent to which groups implement equal opportunities and challenge discrimination in their activities

- extent of accountability of groups to their own members and neighbourhoods

- extent and nature of links and good working relationships between groups for joint working and combined initiatives

- extent of links and involvement of groups with agencies and the Council in joint planning of local services and new strategic initiatives

- extent to which groups lead on projects and control assets in the community.

Each question in the checklist printed in Part Seven, Resource One relates to these features. We now have a look at the questions in relation to this set of features, using the four themes to divide the questions into categories.

Questions 1 to 8

These are introductory questions that should give useful basic information, particularly on **Aims and Activities** and type of people the group works with. The answers given under activities can be analysed for common features. See the example overleaf from the Bradford New Deal for Communities.

BUILDING ORGANISATIONS
(Questions 9 to 35)

Question 9: this grid contains questions to find out about **Problems** that groups are facing. The last question within the grid is open ended and needs plenty of space for the response. The response to question 9 could be cross-tabulated with different types of groups to find out if there is a pattern for particular problems being experienced by particular types of groups.

Question 10 relates specifically to **Achievements**. This question asks about positive achievements of the last two years. It is useful to recognise and value these in the profile's description of the area.

Question 11: if many groups have only been established recently, it is likely they will generally have less experience than well-established ones.

Questions 12 to 15: these questions give an idea of how large the groups are and how many active members they have. If an area has many large groups with a substantial membership, with more than just two or three active organisers, it is a sign of more activity than an area with only a few small groups dependent on just one or two key leaders.

Question 16 relates to **Structure**: this asks about whether the group has a constitution. Without a constitution, groups are unlikely to be able to receive grant aid. A constitution helps a group become more accountable to its membership and neighbourhood. Consequently, if a large number of the groups in a neighbourhood lack a constitution, this could be seen as a sign of a lower level of organisation.

This question also asks if groups are constituted as charities or companies. Groups that have such structures are generally better placed to take on new funding, develop new projects and build an asset base. The existence of co-operatives, community enterprise and generated income from trading are all signs of local enterprise and potential for further growth. A co-operative is a group with formal rules in which all members are involved as equal partners, but it may not always be very accountable to the local area.

Be aware that some groups will need to circle more than one box to answer this question because they could be, for example, both a limited company and registered charity.

Questions 17 to 21: these ask about **Management committees** and leadership within the group. If the majority of groups in the area do not have a management committee but are led by one or two probably overworked individuals, it is grounds for some concern.

Questions 22 to 24 ask about Money.

The Bradford New Deal for Communities Survey

Findings: activities

It is useful to get a general idea of the range of activities these 25 community and voluntary groups surveyed are involved in:

- 3 groups provide advice
- 11 organise social activities
- 4 provide advocacy services
- 8 are concerned with worship or religious education
- 6 are involved in community education or training
- 1 group is concerned with sports
- 1 is working with young people
- 6 are aimed at older people
- 1 provides parent education
- 3 are involved in arts activities
- 5 promote cultural awareness

We know that 8 groups are active in their immediate neighbourhoods only, 3 are active throughout the whole New Deal for Communities area, and 12 work in a wider area in the district as well.

Eight groups have existed for 5 years or less but another 8 groups have been going for over 20 years. This shows there is a wealth of experience to draw on – and some new groups are emerging.

Question 22: this concerns the sources of **Funding** the group has. Groups that are accessing a variety of sources are likely to be in a stronger position than those that are dependent a single source. This is also the case where groups have substantial revenue from trading or contracts. A contract is a formal agreement to provide certain services for money. For example, Social Services might offer a sum of money to an independent community centre to provide a dozen lunch club places. Revenue from trading means earned income from selling goods or services and can include a wide range of activities from selling cakes at stalls to running charity shops. For groups to be able to generate substantial income from trading indicates that they are relatively well organised and there could be potential here to build on for further community enterprise.

Question 24: this concerns the amount of **Money** a group is accessing. Some groups may be resistant about giving this information – as already mentioned, it is crucial that the use of the data collected is made explicit to any group completing the form. A neighbourhood where most groups have less than £1,000 suggests a lower level of community activity than one where many were accessing £100,000 or over. The number of paid staff employed by any one group would also be a similar indicator.

Question 27 is about **Premises**: this asks about the buildings/premises which groups use. Generally speaking, groups that own their own building can be seen as better placed than those only able to meet in a member's front room. However, this generalisation will depend on the type of group – a health support group may quite appropriately meet in a member's house and not want to be burdened down with owning or running its own premises. While bearing this in mind, if the survey revealed that the majority of groups only ever met in private houses or public places, this could be seen as limiting their ability to grow and be more secure in their activities. Groups may themselves indicate any problems they have with their premises in Question 28.

Bradford New Deal for Communities Survey

Findings: money issues

- Funding is regarded as a 'significant problem' for 15 out of the 25 groups
- 11 groups have below £10,000 income per year, 7 of these under £1,000
- 19 groups in total have an income of less than £20,000 a year
- Only 2 groups have national lottery funding
- 6 groups obtain funding from other charities
- 6 groups obtain funding from the local authority, though for five of these the amount is under £20,000
- 3 obtain financial support from the private sector

- 13 groups get money from their local fundraising
- No groups said they were mainly community enterprises and only one group gets any income from trading
- No groups (who answered the question) have any guaranteed income from funding beyond 2001
- Only 10 groups have received advice in the last year on funding issues
- Most of this advice came from the Council, some from the Health Authority and the Key Fund.

Questions 29 and 30 relate to **Accessibility**: these ask for information on the accessibility of the premises used by the group. This type of information is useful to include in a directory. Both questions need to be asked – for example, buildings with access but no accessible toilets are of limited use to people who use wheelchairs.

Question 31 relates to **Resources**: this asks about access to resources and equipment. Resources which are given free or available from a member can be vulnerable to change. The information gathered from replies to this question can, in combination with questions concerning funding levels, create a useful initial picture of the area in terms of the level of organisation of the community and voluntary sector. Some areas may have few groups, and those that exist have a low level of resources, little experience of training and few links with each other. Other areas, in comparison, may have a large number of groups and many that are well established, with a variety of funding sources, and access to that can act as a basis for future growth.

Question 32: this is about helping other groups. If this information is used in a directory, it is important to check with the group that they are willing for it to be made public.

Questions 33 to 35 ask about **Action plans**.
Many funders nowadays are requiring groups to develop an action or business plan in order to receive larger amounts of grant aid. Groups that have produced them will have reached a certain level of planning and have a greater chance of accessing funding.

Bradford New Deal for Communities Survey

Findings: premises

- Securing adequate premises is a significant problem for 8 groups.
- 14 groups see 'access to resources' such as computers and printers as no problem, 6 see this as a slight or significant problem.
- 12 groups have free use of building space for their activities, but 9 groups have a problem in securing adequate premises.

BUILDING SKILLS
(Questions 36 to 43)

This section of the questionnaire focuses on the ways groups get help with training, and develop the skills, knowledge and confidence of their groups' members.

Question 36: this gives a broad picture of the extent to which the **Skills** of the most active members of the group fulfil the ability of the group to be effective in achieving its aims and carrying out its activities.

Question 37: this concerns **Training** received and learning achieved over the last year. Generally an area where groups are accessing and using training opportunities can be seen as better organised than one where the development of group members' skills is non-existent or at a very low level of activity. Opportunities for learning may be very limited and restricted to training; this is looked at in question 39.

Question 38 asks about factors that are important in taking up training. The information gathered from this question can be useful to plan training provision.

Questions 41 to 43 ask about **Getting outside advice**: Question 41 finds out about professional advice the group may be receiving that could help it in its organisational development. Some groups make good use of advisors, information officers, consultants and community workers, and this can have a significant impact on the group's structure and ability to respond to new opportunities. Question 43 helps to identify why this may not be accessed.

Bradford New Deal for Communities Survey

Findings: Building skills

- 11 groups out of the 25 had received training in the last year, and 15 said they would like help identifying their training needs
- 13 groups stated they have a slight or significant problem with lack of skills among members for the group to carry out its work effectively
- 8 groups see access to training as no problem but 11 saw this as either a slight or significant problem (6 replied 'don't know' or gave no response to this question)
- Over the last year the range of subjects training groups participated in included: basic food hygiene, first aid, computer skills, management committee skills, marketing, fundraising, counselling and community work, working with children and young people, visioning and planning
- About a third of all groups develop their members learning through sharing skills with others, visits to other centres/groups/projects. Only two groups were using mentoring or secondments.

BUILDING EQUALITY
(Questions 44 to 50)

The capacity or strengths of an area's community organisations will be reflected partly in their ability to base their activities on the principle of equality. This may be shown by the existence of an equal opportunities statement or policy but in some cases groups may be implementing equal opportunities without a written basis to it. For example, a tenants' group may be trying really hard to ensure that young people have a voice on their estate. This may be identified in the more open-ended questions within the building equality section of the questions checklist. Merely having a policy or statement, as asked in Question 44, will not be enough. It obviously needs to be put into action and preferably some monitoring of its progress set up by the group. An area with many groups that both have written policies and are taking action could be seen as being at a higher level of community organisation. Bear in mind that there are some community groups which are appropriately only open to specific people, e.g., Asian women's groups. The group itself can be taking action to increase participation of all members of that particular group and to challenge discrimination more widely in the community.

Statements on equal opportunities

Here are three different forms:

A constitution with a statement within it
Many constitutions say that membership is open to anyone in the chosen area, regardless of age, gender, ethnic origin, religion, etc. Some commit the organisation to applying equal opportunities to all its work.

An equal opportunities statement
Groups often adopt a short equal opportunities statement, which they might pin up on the wall of the office, print in their newsletter or just attach to the constitution. These are often no more than a couple of paragraphs and typically make a general statement like those mentioned above, and state that certain types of behaviour will not be tolerated from staff, members or users, for example racist remarks.

An equal opportunities policy
Longer than a statement, these could cover 2 to 20 pages. They are much more detailed and often include specific details on what actions will be taken to ensure equal opportunities, for example, in staff recruitment.

Bradford New Deal for Communities Survey

Findings: Building equality

- 12 groups have an equal opportunities policy, and 4 have a statement on equality
- Access to childcare is a significant problem for 7 groups
- 10 of the premises used by groups are accessible to people who use wheelchairs, and 6 are partially accessible
- Only 4 groups have all of the building space they use with accessible toilets for people who use wheelchairs, 6 have some, 13 have none. These figures are low, in terms of effective access, for people who use wheelchairs to buildings used by community groups in the area

- Very few groups show signs of implementing or monitoring equal opportunities in any systematic way; the answers to these questions were vague and mostly anecdotal. 'Everybody welcome.' The answers did, however, often convey commitment and concern about these issues.

BUILDING INVOLVEMENT
(Questions 51 to 60)

These questions relate to how people in the area are involved in the group, and how the group itself is consulted by and involved with larger agencies and organisations.

Question 51: this asks about **Accountability** of the group towards its own members and/or users. Some groups are well organised with properly organised annual general meetings, regular feedback meetings and newsletters to communicate with members. Others are separated from their own area, out of touch with what people want, and rarely distribute information to members. Interpreting this type of information will need sensitivity to the type of group; for example, a support group would not be expected to hold an AGM.

Question 53: this concerns **Joint work** with different types of organisations. This may reveal a particular pattern. Groups in the area may have been involved extensively in joint work with the Council but not at all with each other. Or there may be a lack of any joint working, with all organisations concerned working independently. Extensive experience of joint working would indicate a community sector that is more likely to be able to respond to the demands of joint working often associated with European funding and the management of regeneration projects.

Questions 54 to 59: these also ask about **Links** to other groups via networks. Generally, groups that are linked to other groups in some way – through a network or federation – can be seen as stronger than those that remain isolated and out of touch with wider networks. It is assumed that through such links, groups will be better informed than groups that are isolated.

Bradford New Deal for Communities Survey

Findings: Building involvement

Nearly half of all groups have problems in recruiting and training volunteers. This may relate to the relatively low level of voluntary involvement described earlier.

In what ways are groups accountable to their communities and/or users?
- 6 said through newsletters, 8 through representatives on the management committee, 14 through consultation meetings and 12 through less structured forms of contact 'talking to members' etc. The figure of 14 groups using consultation meetings to be accountable seems high.

How does the group find out about the needs of the local community and/or users?

• The majority of groups did not answer this question. However from those that did, we know 4 groups have used a questionnaire to find out about local needs, 7 carry out 'outreach' and 10 find out through meetings.

Who has the group been involved with in joint work over the last year, such as running a play-scheme, organising a new project, etc?

• Again many groups did not complete this question. From those that did answer it, we know that 8 have worked jointly with other community organisations, 6 with voluntary sector organisations or charities, 6 with the Council, and 3 with other statutory organisations, 5 with other organisations.

The level of support survey questions

We now describe in a similar way how to interpret the information gathered from the support organisations checklist of questions given in Resource Two. As described in our Introduction, this type of support can be identified through the following features:

• the range of support organisations active in the area

• the level of advice, resources, funding and facilities provided by these support organisations

• the amount and type of training and capacity building available

• the extent to which capacity building is provided in a planned and co-ordinated manner based on identified needs

• the extent of help provided to groups in developing their own equal opportunities initiatives

• the extent to which support organisations themselves base their activities on equal opportunities

• the level of community work provision in the area

• the role and effectiveness of networks in the area.

Again, each of these features has related questions and all questions are divided into the four themes.

Questions 1 to 10: These provide general information on **Aims, Activities**, area covered and type of groups worked with. This helps to build the picture of the range of support organisations working in the area. A key issue to clarify is the proportion of their activities or services that actually target the area, rather than a wider area or the whole district.

BUILDING SKILLS

Questions 11 to 16: these give useful information on the amount and nature of **Training** available in the area. It also looks at other forms of adult learning such as mentoring. Question 12 asks about **Tailor-made training**. Many community groups prefer such forms of learning, which espccially at early stages of involvement in capacity building, may increase participation. The list in Question 13 shows a range of training issues that many community groups are interested in. Question 14 asks about forms of **Learning provision** other than just training. This is important as capacity building is commonly misunderstood as only including training whereas, in practice, there are a whole variety of ways adults can get involved in learning in a group setting. *Building Community Strengths* (Skinner, 1997) contains an extensive description of these.

Question 17: This asks about the provision of **Advice**. This is specifically about advice for the development of the group – it is not concerned with advice for the individual, such as welfare rights advice.

Bradford New Deal for Communities Survey

Findings: the survey of support organisations

A total of 22 larger organisations and agencies were surveyed to find out about the support they give to the grass-roots groups. These are organisations that are either based in the New Deal for Communities (NDfC) area, or who already work in the area, or who are available to work in the area.

The 22 returned forms from the survey show that:
- 12 organisations work in the whole district, 4 just in the NDfC area
- Only 1 organisation out of 22 works exclusively in its immediate neighbourhood.

This spread of area of activity shows a striking and understandable difference from the pattern shown by the grass-roots community and voluntary groups themselves, which are generally much more neighbourhood and area based.

- 18 out of the 22 organisations provide or organise course-based training for community and voluntary groups
- 12 can provide or organise tailor-made training for groups – training sessions designed particularly for one group
- In terms of the subjects covered, as shown below, there appears to be a reasonable range provided from the checklist provided on the questionnaire form. This checklist of training content is based on research on community groups' training needs in other regions.

Subject of Training	No. of organisations offering training
Publicity	5
Media	6
Money	4
Presentation skills	4
Computer skills	6
Managing staff	3
Managing a building	3
Equal opportunities	7
Fundraising	8
Planning activities	7
Community work skills	7
Evaluation	6
Working as a team	5
Working as a partnership	4
Working with the Council	3
Working with projects and agencies	2
Other	5

Superficially, these figures suggest that there is ample provision of training in the area. However, out of 25 community and voluntary groups in the area, 14 received no training over the last year – the majority. In publicity skills, 16 groups said they have only medium or low-level skills for the needs of their work. Both these points suggest that the training that is available may not be what groups need or may not be advertised well enough in the area. Fifteen groups in the area say they would like help to identify their training needs, and 12 support organisations are offering this service – this shows there is considerable potential to organise training that is more directed at groups' real needs.

BUILDING ORGANISATIONS

Questions 18 to 22: these concern **Money** and **Resources**. The information given in response to Question 18 can be analysed to establish, for example, the time period any one funding source is available for. There may be several effective support organisations based in the area but all of them might provide funding for only the next nine months. Such insecure funding will limit groups' capacity to effectively plan ahead. Question 19 could be very useful information to include in a directory and the use of this information for this purpose is checked in Questions 20 to 22.

Questions 23 and 24: these ask basic, limited questions on **Community work** provision. To identify the number of community workers working in an area is a useful starting point. Community workers can be an important resource for community organisations. An issue to be wary of is that some people confuse community work with working in communities; for example a health promotion worker may be working in communities but not necessarily adopt a community development approach. The second question on roles will help to clarify this, by using the description of what community development consists of provided in this handbook, see p. 8. Further information on community work roles is given in *Building Community Strengths* (Skinner, 1997).

The Bradford New Deal for Communities Survey

Findings

The survey of support organisations identified a wide range of training available for groups as well as many support organisations interested in helping groups to identify their training needs. In practice, however, much of this potential provision was not being taken up locally – many groups simply did not know what was available. Consequently, two of the main recommendations in the action report were that a training forum should be established to co-ordinate provision, and a directory of training be produced.

BUILDING EQUALITY

Questions 25 and 26: these help to provide an outline of support work on equality issues. If the available support is mainly help with writing equal opportunities statements, then it will be limited in its impact. As with other questions, it is useful to compare what support organisations are offering as help with what is actually being used by community and voluntary groups.

BUILDING INVOLVEMENT

Questions 27 to 32: these ask about support to groups on increasing involvement. Question 28 emphasises asking about support to groups in taking action, compared with having a say that is asked about in Question 29.

Questions 33 and 34: these ask about links and in particular about joint planning of support. This can be a useful indication of how co-ordinated support is in the area.

Questions 35 to 37: These questions are about wider issues of how organisations can broaden their support roles in future. It is useful to know if there is potential for increased support, and what may be the blocks to this being achieved. For the future planning of capacity building, these are key questions.

Bradford New Deal for Communities Survey

Findings

The survey showed that the area had a high number of isolated community groups who are at a basic level of organisation and who are not currently accessing available support. While increased co-ordination and publicity of available support were seen as useful steps to address this, the isolated nature of many of these groups led to the conclusion that more community work provision was needed in the area. This would build on the already effective and skilful community work practice in the area, but increase the level of provision in relation to the identified need. The aim would be to specifically work with isolated groups to increase – where they requested it – their level of use of available support in the area.

From findings to conclusions

The term 'findings' here is being used to refer to factual statements arising from the survey; for example, half the community groups in the area do not have a constitution. This can then lead to a conclusion, which will be an interpretation of the findings; for example, the lack of constitutions in such a large proportion of groups indicates that such groups are not well placed to respond to new funding opportunities, as most funders will require more structure. In interpreting the findings to reach conclusions you will need to consider the following points.

☐ **Conclusions will often involve generalisations**
In some cases there will be exceptions to generalisations made about the findings. For example, a tenants' group may only have 10 members and could be included in a statement that 'many groups in the area suffer from a limited level of involvement from members and users'. However, it may be the case that all 10 members of the tenants group are active! Such a group may be the exception to the general trend in the area. The aim of the findings and the conclusion is to identify overall trends while noting particular special cases and exceptions.

☐ **Small does not always equal low level of organisation, more does not always equal higher**
Small-scale groups may be carrying out their chosen roles very effectively, even on a small budget per group. Equally, just by having more groups or organisations *per se* does not necessarily mean a better-organised community or voluntary sector. A combination of features will need to be considered to draw up a picture of the area. Any one factor on its own should not be taken as indicative in its own right of how organised groups are in an area. It is more a case of looking for evidence concerning a number of features of level of organisation and level of support that can then be combined to build a more reliable picture.

☐ **Each area will have its differences and in particular cultural factors will be important**
A minority group's AGM may bring only a handful of members along, yet the festival event attracts a large number of active members who contribute a tremendous amount of energy and creativity. Different ways of organising groups and involving people need to be considered.

☐ **There may be significant differences between the level of community organisation and the level of support**
It will be useful to compare and contrast these. An area may have a relatively high level of support available but this is not being accessed effectively by groups – a

pattern seen in the Bradford New Deal for Communities case study. It may be for example that available support is not well advertised.

With these points and provisos in mind, the information can be used to build up a general picture of the area's level of organisation and level of support. This general picture is very useful – but effective planning of capacity building needs a more precise form of identification of the baseline position. Part Five is about this.

The Community Strengths Framework
Framework

•5

5 The Community Strengths Framework

We now introduce the Community Strengths Framework, which can be used to identify the level of community strengths. Once the information gathered through the surveys has been through an initial phase of analysis and interpretation, groups and organisations can be invited to comment on the findings. This also involves a process of collectively agreeing the levels of community organisation and support, and identifying action points for the future. This will give groups and organisations a sense of ownership and involvement in the findings and actions arising from the profile.

This participative approach is a key element of the community strengths assessment.

Introducing the framework

The aim of the framework is to provide a way to collectively identify what levels of community organisation and support exist in the neighbourhood. It has also been designed as a tool for action planning. All too often, community profiles are produced which at best are used as a local directory, or at worst sit on shelves gathering dust. The use of the Community Strengths Framework aims to give all the groups and organisations in the area an opportunity to look at the broader picture – the sum of all their contributions – and to get involved directly in planning for change and development.

> The Community Strengths Framework has been adapted from a model developed by COGS on behalf of the South Yorkshire Objective 1 Programme and called 'A Framework for Measuring the Progression of Developing Local Communities'. The principal aims of the original version were to assist the people who live and work in communities to plan an informed local community strategy, and assess their progression and development.

The five levels

The Community Strengths Framework has five levels. Each level can be defined by a series of characteristics, which relate to degrees of community organisation and support. Suggested characteristics of each level are printed in full in Resource Three. Please take a look at them now to get an idea of how the framework actually works. The framework suggests that any one neighbourhood is at a certain level for community organisation, and a certain level for support. These two levels may not necessarily be the same for any one area. For example, the neighbourhood may have a network of well-organised and active community groups, and so be at Level Four for community organisation – but lack adequate support from larger organisations and agencies, and so are at Level Two for support. These levels have each been given a name to summarise the set of characteristics at that level:

Level One: Creating	**Level Two: Connecting**
Level Three: Structuring	**Level Four: Partnering**

Level Five: Sustaining

The framework can be used to review the findings from the two surveys to assess the levels at which the neighbourhood is at. In other words, it can help to assess whether a neighbourhood is primarily at the creating, connecting, structuring, partnering or sustaining phase of development. The survey findings can be related to particular characteristics in the framework.

The four themes

The framework is also divided into categories based on the four key themes which were introduced earlier for use in the surveys:

- Building organisations
- Building skills
- Building equality
- Building involvement.

In combination, using themes and levels can help to identify the overall pattern for a neighbourhood.

By including the four themes, there is the scope to acknowledge that community organisation in the neighbourhood may be at Level One for building skills but Level Three for building organisations and so on. It can also address the same issues for the support organisations. They may also be at different levels for different themes. In theory, eight different features could be identified as follows:

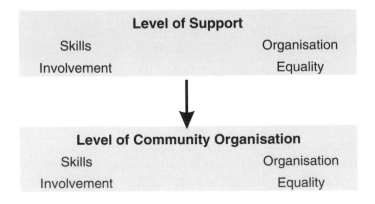

In practice it is unlikely that such a high level of detail will be necessary, but the Community Strengths Framework has the potential to be used in this precise manner where needed.

The full framework printed in Resource Three illustrates the whole range of potential characteristics, and includes a checklist of 'milestones' for possible future actions. It can be used in its entirety or adapted to include specific local characteristics, relevant to the surveys' findings.

It is recognised that community activity is complex – some community and voluntary groups will be further on than others in terms of, for example, experience of partnership working. But even with such variation, the surveys' findings are likely to generate an overall view of where the neighbourhood can be placed in the framework.

Planning for action

The five levels can form the baseline for future planning and action. The framework adopts an outcome-based approach to assist neighbourhoods to build on their strengths. It includes a range of ways to move from a low level of community organisation to more active involvement and ownership of resources. It is important that all groups and agencies based in the neighbourhood should be given the opportunity to consider such future action. This process for planning action is carried out through the workshop described on p. 66.

A summary of the framework is given overleaf. This is a brief introduction to the levels – it combines both the level of organisation, and levels of support. The possible actions given in each case are only examples to give you the flavour of what could be needed – please see the Action Points in Resource Four for a fuller range of options.

Using the framework

There needs to be opportunities for all local community groups and support organisations to be involved fully in identifying the levels for the area, and in proposing what should happen next. In order to do this, it is essential that at least one open workshop event is held. All groups and support organisations identified as being active in the area should be invited to participate, as well as partnerships and other key agencies and organisations.

In addition, it is useful to hold some focus groups targeted at particular types of people, for example, at members of smaller community and voluntary groups. It may also be useful to hold a separate focus group for support organisations, or for community groups who face particular barriers to involvement, such as disabled people's groups, and black and minority ethnic groups. The focus groups can act as a 'taster' session, encouraging involvement in the larger workshop. In this way the focus groups can help to collect additional information for the profile as well as produce greater overall participation in the workshop. They need to be held in the few weeks running up to the main workshop event.

Community Strengths Framework: summary table

	Theme	Level 1 Creating	Level 2 Connecting	Level 3 Structuring	Level 4 Partnering	Level 5 Sustaining
BUILDING ORGANISATION	Baseline	Few active community groups, low level of co-ordinated activity, little external support	Some established groups and new ones emerging, increasing resources available from support agencies	Groups and agencies understand and aim to maximise their own organisational capacity	There is a strategic approach to joint working between the majority of groups and agencies based in the area	Highly organised community groups and infrastructure. Support agencies are fully accountable to those they service
	Possible action	Increase activity and involvement	Develop information and networking between groups	Develop infrastructures which are locally accountable	Develop active partnerships	Develop sustainable community-led projects, partnerships and policies
BUILDING SKILLS	Baseline	Few opportunities for, and low take-up of, relevant and accessible training	Some awareness of training and learning opportunities but many unacknowledged barriers	Support, training and learning opportunities are well organised	Wide range of skills and skill sharing amongst community groups. Agencies provide relevant and flexible training packages	Training needs and training opportunities are frequently reviewed and addressed
	Possible action	Identify existing skills and training gaps	Develop opportunities for sharing skills and knowledge	Develop locally relevant training courses and recognition for learning through action	Analyse the existing relationship between skills development and community strengths – plan for the future with local partners	Ensure continual access to learning opportunities
BUILDING EQUALITY	Baseline	Little awareness and knowledge about different community needs and perspectives	Some evidence of equal opportunities policies being implemented	Increase in equal opportunities action plans. Networks reflect a variety of interests and perspectives	There are integrated strategies to promote greater access and involvement	Minority and marginalised groups have equal access to strategic planning processes
	Possible action	Increase knowledge and awareness of community diversity	Share best practice	Target under-represented groups and promote access and inclusion	Develop strategic action to ensure all community members benefit from activities	Regularly review and address barriers to involvement
BUILDING INVOLVEMENT	Baseline	Little involvement in community groups. Only a few groups contribute to planning processes	Community groups are growing. There are some consultation procedures in place.	Significant active membership of community groups. Clear processes for decision making	There is support for community action. There is increasing control of local services/agencies	Community groups play recognised and equal roles in local planning and development
	Possible action	Bring groups together and share strengths	Publicise and develop consultation mechanisms	Develop accountable and representative structures	Ensure community participation strategies across all sectors	Provide continuing support for community-led developments

More detailed information on how to organise the workshop and focus groups is provided in Resource Five. The aim in this section is to describe more generally the overall role of the workshop in relation to the framework.

Organising the workshop

The main aims of the workshop are to:

• gather more information from participants

- share the information gathered from the surveys and present the initial findings
- check the key findings with participants
- use the framework to collectively agree on the levels of community organisation
- agree on the levels of support
- begin to identify steps for future development.

The workshop format needs to enable everyone to learn and contribute. It will therefore need a participatory style, led by people who have good facilitation skills. What follows is an introduction to the main elements of the workshop.

Gathering more information from participants

This is particularly information about people's perceptions of the area and their degree of confidence that change can really happen. It is collected through the workshop because it is more appropriate than the surveys for this type of information. Methods for doing this are described in Resource Five.

Presenting and checking the findings

The main findings and conclusions from the two surveys can be presented in a lively and accessible manner, where possible using visual aids. Separating the information out into the two broad categories of community organisation, and support, will help to clarify the key findings. Using the four themes also helps to break the findings up into bite-size chunks. Discussion and debate can be invited on the findings. This process may add new perspectives and minority views, which should be carefully noted to be included in the final report. Any key ideas and proposals from the focus groups can be fed in at this point.

Bradford New Deal for Communities

Community profile workshop

The workshop held in the Bradford New Deal for Communities area involved 40 people, representing a broad cross-section of organisations including community groups, projects, voluntary organisations, agencies, the local authority and the Bradford Trident Partnership. After debate and discussion of the main findings, the framework was introduced on posters displayed around the room. Participants clearly identified the level of community organisation for the area for three of the four themes as at Level Two. However, for Building equality the pattern was less clear, though with an emphasis in Level Three. Two focus group meetings were also held, each targeted at community groups and support organisations.

Collectively identifying the levels of community organisation

The framework itself now needs to be introduced. The five levels of community organisation can be presented on large sheets of card or paper. These sheets can act as posters: each poster contains the text on one theme of the framework from one particular level. You will find that the framework printed in the Resources Section has been designed in a way that is easy to photocopy and enlarge for this purpose. The posters can be in different colours – to distinguish between the four themes – and displayed in different parts of the room. An introduction to the different levels and themes is needed, perhaps with one or two examples.

All participants can then be invited to assess the level their area is at for each of the four themes, combining both their own experience and views on the area with the information provided through the surveys' findings. This can be done through a process of choice during the workshop. The simplest way to do this – which is also good fun – is where each participant is given four coloured stickers. Each participant then places their stickers on the posters, one sticker per poster, choosing the appropriate level for each theme that they think describes where the area is at. We suggest that this process is only carried out with regard to the level of community organisation. This is because it may be too complicated to repeat the exercise for the level of support, involving too many posters and stickers!

Generally, this exercise will produce a pattern on each theme that demonstrates a collectively-held view of where the neighbourhood is at. This will provide a baseline position for community organisation for each of the four themes. There may be significant differences between the views of the groups and the support organisations about this, and each of the two sectors can be given different coloured stickers to identify if this is the case. If there is a divergence of views, space will need to be created to discuss the basis of any differing perceptions and to try to identify some common ground.

Agreeing on the levels of support

The workshop should include some debate on the proposed levels of support in relation to each of the four themes. Proposals on these arising from the findings can be presented by the facilitators at this point, and discussed. As suggested above, repeating the process of collectively choosing the levels may be too complicated – it depends partly on the amount of time available. Either way, an agreed view needs to be reached that identifies the levels of support for each of the four theme areas. An overall summary can now be obtained of the levels of support and community organisation.

Beginning to plan for action

There may be a consensus to remain at the present level identified for each theme or there might be agreement to aim for the next level. Where some further action and development is agreed on, a useful exercise to carry out at this point is to ask all participants to divide into four different theme groups and identify what needs to happen to help move the area for each particular theme from its existing level to the next level up. The posters can be used to help this process. There is a more detailed listing of suggested activities linked to the four themes in Resource Five. These actions are designed to be carried out by local groups, agencies, networks and partnerships to reach the next level. This listing is not comprehensive and will obviously need to be adapted to local needs but it will help in the workshop, and in any later planning activities, to prompt and think through ideas for the future. The points fed back from these theme groups can then be shared with all the other participants and included in the draft report. The workshop will need to finish with a summary of all the main points, the proposals agreed on, and an outline of the next steps involved in completing the community profile. This involves producing an action report and is described in Part Six.

General points about using the framework

As you can see, this is a highly participatory approach to using the framework. This approach is important for two reasons:

- by involving a broad cross-section of groups and organisations, it ensures the identification of levels is based on local knowledge and people's real experiences of living and working in the area, in combination with the survey data

- involving groups and organisations in this process is also important to create a sense of ownership in planning for future development and change. It means people have had a real opportunity to have a say and to see that their views have been debated and considered.

In using and interpreting the framework, please bear in mind the following points:

- **The framework is not intended to be prescriptive**
  It should not be assumed that neighbourhoods should always strive to reach a higher level. Equally, the framework is not intended to undermine existing community strengths but to recognise them and build upon them. If the majority of groups in the neighbourhood decide to keep to the existing level there should not be external pressure to drive it upwards.

- **Using the framework is not an exact science**
  It involves an element of subjective assessment. The levels contain reference, fairly frequently to 'few', 'some', 'several', as it is not possible to give clear guidance on likely numbers. This is not necessarily a problem as the quality of service provision and effectiveness of community action is perhaps more important than numbers of groups or support organisations *per se*.
  The key safety net to limiting the potential subjectivity of your own interpretation is the highly participative approach to the community strengths assessment. A broad cross-section of groups and organisations, through focus groups and the workshop, will contribute to and comment on the assessment of levels using their own daily frontline experience of living and working in the area. In practice, you will find in most cases there will be a clearly held majority view on the levels – reflected in the pattern of stickers on posters.

- **The framework can be used and adopted creatively**
  It provides a model of capacity building that has the potential to be used in a wide variety of ways. It could, for example, be used as a checklist to help any one organisation or group to take stock of its own particular levels within the four

themes. It could also be adopted to relate to the needs of communities of interest that may be spread across a district, rather than concentrated in a geographical area. The whole process of carrying out a community profile could start by building a vision of the future in a neighbourhood through open planning sessions with local groups, using the levels to identify where people would ideally be – then carry out the surveys to identify the current reality … Please adapt it to your needs – it's not written on tablets of stone!

Planning for action

6 Planning for action

Part Six is about action. A key issue is to ensure the assessment is integrated into the planning of new initiatives and strategies. We look at how to use community strengths assessments in planning for action, and touch on a range of other options arising from use of the framework. We also focus on the needs of areas involved in major regeneration programmes and the process involved in producing a strategy for capacity building. Part Six finishes with a general review of community strengths profiling in the context of a community development approach.

Producing the action report

Planning for action can be carried out in a variety of ways. A useful first step is to produce a report with an emphasis on action. The content of the report can be based on the following sources:

- the main findings from the surveys

- agreed recommendations and proposals made during the focus groups and the workshop, especially those based on how the area can move between levels

- additional useful and appropriate points taken from the action checklist provided in Part Seven, Resource Four

- your own additional perspectives and conclusions arising from the work on the surveys.

The surveys and workshop will have helped to identify the levels at which the area is currently situated for each of the four themes of Building skills, Building organisations, Building involvement and Building equality. The action points contained in Resource Four are intended to be examples to stimulate strategic thinking in relation to the four themes.

The first draft of the report could be presented to the network, steering group or partnership body that originally gave its backing for the profile to be carried out. In particular, any recommendations from the workshop will need to be looked at and hopefully approved as the basis for action and the way forward. Following this initial discussion, the draft report could then be circulated to all known public sector organisations, agencies and groups in the area, as well as community workers and ward members, for comment before a final version is printed. This final round of consultation may seem excessive, but it is important to ensure that all stakeholders have a chance to comment and contribute. Strongly held views that are different from the main recommendations, could then be debated by the steering group and, if not agreed on, at least noted in the final report.

Bradford New Deal for Communities Profile

Producing the action report

Following the workshop and focus groups, a draft report was drawn up. This included all the points for action agreed on at the workshop as well as the data and findings arising from the two surveys. A draft version of the report was circulated to the board members of Bradford Trident and presented to the partnership's Youth, Education and Community Involvement Working Group. With their support it was then circulated to all known groups and organisations in the area as well as key community workers, local politicians and appropriate council officers. Comments were received, minor amendments made and the final version printed.

Integration into planning

At this point there is the possibility that the report is simply filed away! As an alternative to this, we now describe ways in which the community strength assessment can be developed and integrated into the planning of projects, services and strategies.

Planning local projects

The community strengths assessment can be used to inform the setting up of new community development projects in the area. Use of existing budgets from a regeneration partnership, agency or local authority will be more effectively employed where the design of the project considers the baseline levels. Equally, bids for additional or new funding sources, such as trusts and special government schemes, can be strengthened by basing the application on the detailed local knowledge the profile can provide.

Planning the provision of community work

The community strengths assessment can contribute to a review of community work in the area. The profile itself will provide a useful context to such a review. The profile could be further developed into an audit of community work that finds out more precise information on the range and nature of community work provision.

Planning local services

The community strengths assessment can help service providers – whether local authority, voluntary sector or agencies – to plan their activities in the neighbourhood. Increasingly, service providers, through initiatives such as Best Value, are committed to engaging local communities in decision-making and contributing to prioritising use of resources. In some areas of service provision, such as health, consulting and involving users and communities is reflected in nationally-set targets. Consequently, the findings and recommendations will be useful not just to support organisations. The draft report can be used as a basis for discussion with local partnerships, with appropriate service managers and with ward members from the local authority.

The art of planning

How any proposed action is integrated into planning services, support, initiatives and projects will vary in each case depending on local circumstances. Over time changes in local circumstances may affect the levels of community organisation. For example, key community group leaders may move and leave a gap in local skills and knowledge or perhaps a space to develop new initiatives. Equally, there may be external change initiated outside the local area that needs to be catered for: an example is new central government policies such as neighbourhood management that influence the direction and sustainability of communities. There may also be technical changes that affect how communities work – such as global increase in access to technology and use of the Internet, which is changing the way people learn and communicate. Some of this change can be anticipated, some cannot, but any forward planning will need to consider how robust groups and organisations are, the different roles they might play in the future, and the different relationships they might form. In other words, advance planning needs to consider what key changes are in the pipeline from known internal and external sources – but be firmly based on an assessment of the level of community organisation as a baseline starting point.

Planning capacity building

Where appropriate, the final report for the community strengths profile can be further developed and broadened into a strategy for capacity building for the area. Particularly in areas involved in or about to be involved in major regeneration programmes, such as New Deal for Communities, Neighbourhood Renewal or European Structural funds, this will be useful to specifically address many of the issues and concerns of local groups and other key stakeholders in the regeneration process.

The capacity building strategy will need to consider the following elements, some of which will already be in the action report:

- a description of the needs of the voluntary and community groups, divided into the four themes

- a description of the current support provided, divided into the four themes

- the overall community strategy or regeneration strategy for the whole city/district

- the local regeneration strategy and delivery plan, if they already exist, for the specific area

- the type of activities and support that capacity building in this area needs to include for community and voluntary groups

- the type of activities and support that capacity building in this area needs to include for larger organisations, agencies and partnerships

- consideration of the balance between expanding the support provided by existing organisations or directing resources into new projects

- a time frame, a clear set of objectives and a range of targets

- a clear statement of how it will be funded, the range of sources to be used and the level of funding required for its effective implementation.

The development of an area-based strategy for capacity building is an essential element of any regeneration programme. Many funders and government policymakers now accept this basic position. To be effective, the capacity building strategy will need to be fully recognised within the main regeneration strategy and allocated adequate funding and resources.

What is equally important is that capacity building is recognised as important for larger organisations and agencies. Many front line staff are now involved in working with communities and are often untrained, and unsupported. Equally managers are supervising such staff and involved in partnerships and joint planning initiatives yet may be lacking the knowledge and conceptual base to inform their work. Organisational structures and practices also need to be carefully looked at to ensure they are appropriate for the effective support and involvement of communities. Further information on many of these issues and in particular, the range of activities that capacity building can include is available (Skinner, 1997).

A definition of capacity building

A commonly used definition of community capacity building is:

'Development work that strengthens the ability of community organisations to build their structures, support, people and skills so that they are better able to define and achieve their objectives and engage in consultation and planning, manage community projects and take part in partnerships and community enterprises.This development work organised in a way that reflects the principles of community development.'

(Skinner, 1997, pp. 1–2)

Key features of this definition are that:

- it emphasises a 'bottom up' approach, that is focusing on the needs of grass-roots community organisations
- it addresses both skills and structures, that is how such community organisations are organised and can be strengthened
- it addresses the support available to the community organisations, such as resources, advice and facilities
- it is concerned with community capacity building rather than economic capacity building, which would primarily address economic outcomes
- it is clear in incorporating community development principles, such as equality.

It needs to be complemented by capacity building that addresses the development needs of agencies and larger organisations so that they can increase their ability to work with community and voluntary groups.

Strategic planning at city/district level

Different organisations and agencies are joining together increasingly at city/district level to form strategic partnerships. This development nationally is being promoted by central government through both the Neighbourhood Renewal initiative and the statutory requirements concerning community planning. Increasingly, local strategic partnerships will be taking the lead in co-ordinating and facilitating neighbourhood development and locality planning. In this context, what is the potential contribution of community strengths assessments?

It is recommended that the Local Strategic Partnership in each city/district adopts a rolling programme of community strengths profiles – to build up a picture over time of community strengths among a range of neighbourhoods. This stock of profiles would mean that regeneration initiatives could be planned more systematically, with much greater awareness of what support is needed in different areas to achieve real change. The baselines of capacity identified across the city/district may well reveal significant differences that may need different types of regeneration priorities and different types of capacity building provision.

This concept of a rolling programme of community strengths profiling is an exciting idea that many local strategic partnerships and communities may be interested in adopting. Achieving this will need a coherent and organised policy that a wide range of stakeholders support. It will also, in each area, need the explicit backing of the majority of local groups, without which it is not advisable to proceed.

Many cities/districts across Britain have a number of areas identified as displaying high levels of deprivation compared to the national average (Social Exclusion Unit, 2000). Typically, in any one city/district, several of these areas will already have a regeneration programme in place, while others may be identified as priority areas for future funding schemes as they come on stream, for example funds to be delivered through the Neighbourhood Renewal Programme.

The rolling programme will produce community strengths profiles that may have different roles depending on the stage the area is at regarding investment in regeneration programmes and initiatives. Here are four possibilities:

- **Prior to the start of the programme**

  An area may have been prioritised to receive the next round of available regeneration scheme funding based on the assessment of indicators of local deprivation. A community strengths profile carried out at this point can be very useful to inform the process of preparation and the first few years of the main regeneration scheme. In the year prior to the main programme starting, preparatory work can be done. This work will itself need resources allocated in a planned and coherent manner.

  If capacity is at a low baseline in such an area before the start of a major regeneration programme, it may also mean the first one or two years of the regeneration programme need to focus especially on building such capacity. Reaching the appropriate level of community organisation can consequently be part of the objectives of the first phase of the regeneration programme (Lloyd, 1996). This approach is increasingly recognised as a key element of regeneration programmes and has been specifically built into the new programme of Objective Two European structural funds.

- **At the start of the regeneration programme**

  Increasingly, the pattern of a limited number of areas being prioritised for regeneration schemes leaving a further short list of excluded areas is being overturned by the new thinking associated with Neighbourhood Renewal. Community profiles carried out at the start of regeneration initiatives in several areas simultaneously has the advantage that resources for this can be built into the use of funds in a strategic manner. The funding of such year one baseline assessments has been increasingly endorsed by mainstream funding programmes – for example, the European Objective Two funds.

- **At a mid-way point during the programme**
  Many regeneration programmes will have been set up without properly considering the issue of community capacity but as the scheme progresses, this need becomes more pressing. This may be especially so as community representatives become more assertive in expressing what is needed to support effective community involvement. A mid-way community profile will be very useful to stock take on the position and the programme's priorities may be able to be amended in the light of this. Some discussion with the regional development agency or government office would be helpful at an early stage to ensure this initiative will receive a supportive response. However, a mid-way point should not be planned for as an alternative to the point at the start of the programme and can not be seen as a substitute.

- **Near the end point of the programme**
  This is also a key to achieving sustainability of the regeneration investment to ensure that skills and structures are in place for some form of continuation of the initiative. If a community strengths profile was also carried out at an earlier point, this final year assessment could be a useful form of evaluation. Resources may need to be allocated for this to ensure a positive response can be made to the findings.

These four main opportunities have varying advantages and disadvantages. Generally, however, leaving it to the mid-way or near the end of the programme is simply too late. The first two options provide scope for effective planning and response to identified needs.

A further option is to repeat the community strengths profile process in each area after a certain period of time in order to assess progress in achieving change and movement between levels. This may be, for example, after three or five years. Compared to the baseline position, the area may have shifted up levels in some particular theme areas, remained stationary or even moved downwards. This type of review would act as a form of evaluation of capacity building at a strategic level and could help to ensure real progress is being made. The repeat profile would need to take account of any major external changes affecting the area that may affect the validity of the comparison.

Bradford New Deal for Communities

The Bradford Trident Partnership's working group on youth, education and community approved the community strengths action report in full and is committed to using the recommendations in an active way to inform and influence decision-making. They are also committed to repeating the profile process at a future point to fully assess the impact of new initiatives being developed in relation to the findings.

The potential misuse of community strengths profiles

A key concern is how community strengths profiles are used in the process of prioritising between potential regeneration areas. Many cities and districts, through their local authorities and local strategic partnerships, are developing systematic approaches to the prioritisation of neighbourhoods for future allocation of resources available through major regeneration programmes. In this context, there is the possibility that community strengths profiles and the baseline information they provide could be used in a very top-down way to influence the choice of area prioritised for the next available round of regeneration funding. This would obviously be complementary to the assessment, based on recommended indicators such as the Index of Local Deprivation.

The authors of this publication specifically request that community strengths profiles are not used to prioritise areas in this way. **This is for two reasons:**

- first, they may distort the information collection process and agreement on the levels of development, given that this is identified in a very participative manner and that participants may want to present their area in a very positive light. This may rightly or wrongly arise from the perception that areas that are at a very low baseline point of community organisation and support will not be prioritised for major funding schemes until they develop their capacity

- secondly, there is the concern that the whole process of carrying community strengths profiles will become dominated by the funding agenda and will be seen as a gateway through which to pass, rather than as a tool to more broadly increase funding and resources in the area.

The potential use of community strengths profiles with communities of interest

Community strengths profiles can be adapted for use in and with groups who may be spread across a city, district or region rather than are concentrated in one area. This could, for example, be disabled people's groups or a particular minority ethnic group. The adaptation of the surveys may need to consider the following points:

- [ ] personal visits to groups may be more difficult when longer distances are involved, especially in rural areas
- [ ] there may be particular political and cultural issues to be aware of, and sensitive to, when contacting groups
- [ ] building the list of support organisations may be more complicated if groups are spread around a whole city or district and could potentially be supported by a larger number or wider range of organisations
- [ ] bringing people together for the participative workshop may require more planning and support.

Troubleshooting

This handbook, which is fundamentally practical in its aims, will by now have – we hope! – provided you with a clear idea of how to organise and carry out a community strengths assessment. In carrying out the practical work of coordinating the assessment, it is worth being aware of several potential pitfalls. The following points give some indication on how to reduce or avoid the potential problem:

- **The assessment is dominated by an external agenda**
  Community strengths profiles involve a key early stage of consultation and local involvement. If, through this process, the majority of local groups do not want to participate or give their support, we recommend that the proposal to carry out the assessment is dropped. Forcing it on an area that does not want it will only create bad feeling and no doubt achieve a low level of response.

- **Local groups feel excluded from the process**
  A second possibility, despite the best of intentions and strong local backing, is that local groups still become divorced from the work of the assessment. Having a steering group with local representatives, employing local people to carry out the surveys, holding open meetings on updates and some form of regular communication on progress all help to ensure close contact and support. Forming a local steering group should, as long as it is broadly representative, help to increase the response rate to the survey, especially as it is a way of building up trust and interest in the profile. In some areas, groups may be isolated and mistrustful of agencies and the council; the profile may be perceived as a form of external audit to review or reduce funding locally. In such cases, spending time to support and encourage people's involvement in the steering group and being clear about how the information will be used is very important.

- **The assessment loses its clarity of purpose**
  Community strengths assessments are, in practice, very specific and will be, for some people, a new approach to assessing needs in neighbourhoods. It is common, however, that some people do not appreciate the importance of finding out about the needs of groups in an area as opposed to finding out about the needs of individuals. If such a survey is more appropriate to the area, then obviously this could be done instead of or as well as a community strengths assessment. The important point is to be clear at an early stage about what is and what is not being attempted to avoid later confusion.

- **There are not enough resources to carry out the whole community strengths assessment**
  It may be that only limited help is available for the survey work and only parts of the whole assessment can be carried out. In such cases, the first priority is to survey the community and voluntary groups. This is because this grass-roots level of activity is the element often missed out of profiles and is the key to effective and lasting change in communities. The action report in such cases will need to clearly recognise that only part of the picture is given and that the level of support has not been assessed. This will limit its usefulness though producing such a report may well be the basis of obtaining resources for the remaining work.

All these points relate to the need for community strengths profiling to be based firmly on a community development approach.

The future use of the framework

Finally, we present some wider thoughts on the potential future use of the framework. This handbook has described a relatively straightforward method of assessing community strengths, focusing on surveying community and voluntary sector organisations and the level of support. Focusing on these elements has two key advantages:

- it provides a profile method that is manageable in terms of size and scope
- it provides a method that has been tried and tested through pilots.

It needs to be recognised however, that building a more comprehensive picture of community strengths in neighbourhoods would require further information gathering and analysis of a number of additional elements. You will see listed in the community strengths framework some characteristics for which there are no directly related questions in the questions checklists provided in the Resources Sections in Part Seven. This is because we have only included in the scope of the community strengths profile, methods and questions that have been tried and tested through the pilots. In practice, to understand the full scope of community strengths would involve more detailed consideration and assessment of this wider range of characteristics.

These additional elements are summarised as follows:

- **Local leadership** – the role and effectiveness of council members, key local leaders, community champions and activists
- **Local partnerships** – the openness, accountability and effectiveness of locally-based partnerships
- **Networks** – the roles and membership of networks
- **Community work** – the level of provision and effectiveness of locally-based community workers
- **Policies and programmes** – the extent to which policies of large agencies, and the local authority and their major spending programmes provide opportunities to build the capacity of local groups – in addition to those specifically carrying out this role identified in the survey of support organisations.

Some of these elements, described in the Fuller Picture diagram below, are included already in the community strengths assessment – such as networks and community work provision – though in a rather limited manner. Others are barely touched on – such as the effectiveness of local leadership and the role of local partnerships. Each of these is a specialist area and information on further publications that can help to address these issues is given in the Bibliography. For some of these there are already fairly extensive practical guidelines available; in other areas there is a serious lack of existing toolkits. In addition, there may be other factors that need to be considered to complete the picture but these have yet to be identified.

The Fuller Picture: Assessing Community Strengths

The community strengths framework can act as the overall context for assessing these other elements. It already includes reference to them, and it can be developed and extended over time, as more understanding of the role of each of these additional elements is unearthed. In the longer term, there may also be additional elements which further research and fieldwork will identify that will need to be considered to fully assess community strengths.

In summary, it needs to be recognised that community strengths profiling, as described in this publication, has a specific part to play in assessing community strengths and covers only one part – though the crucial part – of the fuller picture of comprehensive community strengths assessments. This is an exciting and growing field of practice and research. The remaining gaps in the picture will be filled as knowledge increases. You can be involved in this yourself by developing and piloting new methods to profile the remaining elements. Methods to assess levels for some of these characteristics are not yet developed, which reflects the fact that community capacity building and community development as disciplines are still in their infancy in Britain. We hope you will join us to develop new methods of community profiling – and share your experience with others so that a stock of tried and tested methods can be built up. In this way we hope communities will be strengthened and empowered at the grass roots.

Resources •7

This handbook has taken you through a process to profile and assess community strengths. We have highlighted the key features and tried to anticipate some of the issues you might face. In this Resources Section, you will find some practical tools to help you undertake the community strengths assessment.

Resource One: The Community Groups Survey Questions

This survey is for collecting information on the level of community organisation.

Introduction

Below is a list of questions that you can use in designing your questionnaire for the survey of community and voluntary groups in your area. In using this list and designing your questionnaire please bear in mind the following points:

- It is unlikely that you will use all the questions provided, as you may then end up with a questionnaire form that is far too long. Use the checklist to decide which mix of questions suit your needs.

- Do not just photocopy this list – it is not a ready-made questionnaire. When designing your own questionnaire form, you will, in many cases, need to increase the space available for the answers. Also, for clarity, ensure any tables are not split between pages.

- Some question options will need either circling (we have used this for our checklist of questions) or what are called tick boxes which look like this: ☐

- Several questions refer to the 'area'. The use of the questions in a survey will consequently need a covering letter or guidelines/map for people completing the form, letting them know what the area covers. Please see Part Two p. 23 for more information on this.

- We have presented some questions, where there is a list of options to respond to, with the label (a) (b) (c) (d) etc. On some of these questions when you are actually inputting the data using a computer programme, you may need to add numbers to each option to replace the existing letters – these are called codes. We suggest you get advice on how to do this from a person with research skills.

Checklist of questions for the survey of community and voluntary groups

Q1. Name of group:

Q2. Address, phone number and email address:

Q3. Main contact name and role (and address if different from above):

Q4. Person completing form (if different from above):

Q5. Please indicate below, the main activities of the group: (*please circle*)

Advice

Arts and cultural activities

Counselling

Housing advice and provision

Resource centre

Self help and support

Training and community education

Other (*please specify*) _____

Advocacy

Campaigning

Environmental activities

Play activities

Social activities

Sports and recreation

Worship and religious education

Q6. Does your group provide services/activities for:

(a) All members of the community?   *If yes, please go to Question 8.*

(b) Only a specific target group in the community,
e.g. lone parents, older people etc.?   *If yes, please go to Question 7.*

(c) Some services for all members of the community,
and some for specific target groups?   *If yes, please go to Question 7.*

Q7. If you provide services for specific groups of people in the community, please indicate below the main groups that you work with or provide services for:
(*please circle any that apply*)

Carers

Ethnic minority groups

(*please specify which ones*) _____

Homeless

Lone parents

Offenders/ex-offenders

People with learning difficulties

People with mental health difficulties

Substance users, e.g. alcohol, drugs, etc

Victims of crime

Women and girls

Children

Families

Lesbian and gay

Low income groups

Older people

People with physical disabilities

People with health concerns

(*please specify*)_____

Unemployed people

Volunteers

Other (*please specify*)_____

Q8. Which part of the district does your group work in/serve? (*please circle*)

(a) Across the area and beyond (including district-wide).

(b) In the whole area only (*see map*).

(c) Local neighbourhood only.

BUILDING ORGANISATIONS

This section is about the development of your group and problems you may be facing.

Problems

Q9. To what extent (if any) are the following issues a problem for the group in meeting its objectives? (*please tick one box for each issue*)

Issue	Significant problem	Slight problem	Occasional problem	No problem	Don't know
Funding					
Managing and keeping staff					
Recruiting and retaining volunteers					
Access to resources, e.g. computers					
Limited skills in the group/organisation					
Access to training for group/organisation to be more effective					
Access to child care for members to join in activities					
Language barriers in communicating with the local community					
Any others: (*please state issues*)					

Achievements

Q10. Please describe some of your group's main achievements over the last two years.

Q11. How many years has the group been active in the area?

Q12. How many members does the group have that live in the area?

Q13. How many of these are active members? (i.e. key members who help to organise or run things)

Q14. In an average week, what is the total number of voluntary hours provided by all your active members in the area? (i.e. the number of hours provided by each member active in the area added together)

Q15. How many people who live in the area use your group's services in an average week? (Please note your total for the week can include people who attend more than once.)

Structure

Q16. Is your group: (*please circle more than one if appropriate*)
   (a) A community group/organisation without constitution
   (b) A community group/organisation with a constitution
   (c) A Limited Company
   (d) A Registered Charity
   (e) A Co-operative
   (f) Trading as a community business/enterprise
   (g) Other (*please specify*) _____

Q17. Does the group have a management committee? (*please circle*)

    (a) Yes   *Please go to Question 18*

    (b) No   *Please go to Question 21*

Q18. Please indicate below if any of the following types of people have the majority of places on the management committee. (*please circle*)

    (a) Council officers

    (b) Local councillors

    (c) Users/members/volunteers

    (d) Paid employees of the group

    (e) Other professionals from other organisations/agencies (e.g. health professionals)

    (f) Other (*please specify*) _____

    (g) No group has a majority.

Q19. How many people are on your management committee?

Q20. On average, how many of these people attend management committee meetings?

                                             Please now go to Question 22

Q21. If there is no management committee, who has overall responsibility for running the group? (*please circle*)

    (a) Individual local resident

    (b) More than one local resident

    (c) Individual paid worker

    (d) More than one paid worker

    (e) Other (*please specify*) _____

Money matters

Q22. Is the group currently funded from any of the following sources? (*please circle all that apply*)

    (a) Central government

    (b) Regeneration partnership

    (c) Local authority

    (d) National Lottery

    (e) Private company

    (f) Charities and other grant aid

    (g) Contract with local authority

    (h) Membership subscriptions

    (i) Local fundraising

    (j) Revenue from trading

    (k) Other sources of income (*please specify*)_____

Q23. For each source given in Q 22 please state for how long the funding is allocated:

(a) _____ (g) _____
(b) _____ (h) _____
(c) _____ (i) _____
(d) _____ (j) _____
(e) _____ (k) _____
(f) _____

Q24. What is the group's approximate income this financial year? (*please circle*)
    (a) Less than £1,000
    (b) £1,000–£9,999
    (c) £10,000–£19,999
    (d) £20,000–£49,999
    (e) £50,000–£99,999
    (f) £100,000 and over

Q25. Does the group employ any paid workers who are working in the area?
    (a) Yes   *Please go to Question 26*
    (b) No   *Please go to Question 27*

Q26. Please indicate the number of paid full-time, part-time and session-based workers employed by your group who are working in the area:

    (a) Total number of paid employees _____
    (b) Number of full-time   _____
    (c) Number of part-time   _____
    (d) Number of sessional staff _____

Q27. What arrangements for using premises does the group have? (*please circle*)
    (a) Ownership of a building
    (b) Shared ownership of building
    (c) Renting a building
    (d) Free use of building
    (e) Only able to meet at a member's home or in a public place
    (f) Other (*please specify*) _____

Q28. What level of satisfaction does your group have with its arrangements for using premises? (*please circle*)
    (a) High satisfaction
    (b) Medium satisfaction
    (c) Low satisfaction

Q29. Are the premises that you use wheelchair accessible? (*please circle*)
    (a) Yes all premises used
    (b) Yes some of the premises used
    (c) No none of the premises used
    (d) Don't know

Q30. Does the building you use have wheelchair accessible toilets? (*please circle*)
    (a) Yes
    (b) No

Q31. To what extent (if any) is access to the following resources a problem for the group/organisation in meeting its objectives? (*please tick one box for each Resource*)

Resource	Significant problem	Slight problem	Occasional problem	No problem at all	Don't know
Meeting space					
Telephone					
Fax					
Desk					
Photocopier					
Computer					
Printer					
Storage					
Internet access					
Transport					

Q32. Do you currently have any of the following facilities or resources available for use by other community groups? (*please tick one box for each Facility/Resource*)

Facility/Resource	Free access	Charge for access	Notes on conditions of use
Telephone			
Fax			
Printer			
Photocopier			
Computer			
Internet			
Meeting Rooms			
Storage			
Transport			
Other (*please add below*)			

Planning activities

Q33. How does your group plan its future work?

Q34. Does the group have an action or business plan?
    (a) Yes   *Please go to Question 35*
    (b) No   *Please go to Question 36*

Q35. How many years does the current action or business plan cover (*please circle*)**?**
    (a) Less than one year
    (b) One to five years
    (c) Over five years

BUILDING SKILLS

This section is about the way your group gets help with training and develops the skills, knowledge and confidence of the group's members.

Q36. *Please think about the skills and experience of the active members of your group, excluding paid staff.* Below is a list of skill areas to which community and voluntary groups often require in order to meet their objectives effectively. **For each of the skill areas listed please indicate the extent to which you agree or disagree with the following statement:**

> **'The skills and experience of our active members fully meet the needs of the organisation in this skill area.'**

Skill area	Strongly agree	Agree	Neither agree nor disagree	Disagree	Strongly disagree	Don't know	Not applicable
Publicity – producing newsletters, leaflets, etc.							
The media – press releases, getting on with the media							
Money – bookkeeping and accounts							
Giving presentations							
Computer skills							
Managing staff							
Managing a building							
Managing projects							
Equal opportunities							
Fundraising							
Planning activities							
Assessing and monitoring the group's work							
Working as a team							
Working in partnerships with other organisation							
How the Council works							
Other (*please specify*)							

Q37. Over the last year, has your group received any training?

    (a) No

    (b) Yes: *please describe below.*

Group members	What training	Where from	*Level of satisfaction (please tick one box)*		
			High	Medium	Low
Staff					
Management committee members					
Volunteers					
Other (*please specify*)					

Q38. Which of the following are important to you in taking up training? (*Please tick*)

	Volunteers and active members	**Committee members**	**Paid staff**
Local venue			
City centre venue			
Accessible venue			
Daytime sessions			
Evening sessions			
Weekend sessions			
Childcare			
Use of community languages			
Sessions for black people			
Sessions for women			
Participative style of training			
Know the trainer already			
Content is tailor made for group's needs			
No cost			
Low cost			
Bursaries/grants available			
Time off for training			
Leads to a qualification			

Q39. Has your group been involved in developing your members' skills through any other kind of activity? (*please circle any that apply*)
(a) Mentoring schemes for members of group
(b) Sharing skills through joint working
(c) Reading books on practical skills for groups
(d) Organising visits or exchanges to centres/projects
(e) Secondments from other organisations to groups
(f) Learning from experience/action
(g) Other (*please describe*)_____

Q40. Would you be interested in getting help with identifying your group's training needs? (*please circle*)
(a) Yes
(b) No

Getting advice

These questions are about the group getting advice and guidance from outside organisations that help it to be better organised.

Q41. Over the last year, has the group had any outside advice? (*please circle any that apply*)
(a) Management issues
(b) Funding advice
(c) Managing money
(d) If other help, please specify where from:
  (e.g. advice on organising events) _____

Q42. Over the last year has the group needed outside advice but not been able to get it? (*please circle*)
(a) Yes
(b) No

Q43. If yes, why was this? (*please describe*) _____

BUILDING EQUALITY

This section is about ways in which your group is trying to help to build equality within your group and in communities.

Q44. Regarding equal opportunities, does your group have: (*please circle*)
(a) A written equal opportunities policy?
(b) A statement of equality within its constitution?
(c) Neither of these

Q45. Please describe how the group is implementing equal opportunities.

Q46. Please describe any ways in which this is being monitored.

Q47. Please indicate any other ways in which your group is taking any action to challenge discrimination: (*please circle any that apply*)
(a) Awareness raising events
(b) Running campaigns
(c) Providing translators/interpreters
(d) Funding equal opportunities initiatives
(e) Other (*please describe*) _____

Q48. Do you get any support from other organisations and agencies for your work on equal opportunities?
(a) Yes   *Please go to Question 49*
(b) No   *Please go to Question 50*

Q49. In general, how satisfied are you with the quality of support you receive on equal opportunities? (*please circle*)
(a) Very satisfied
(b) Satisfied
(c) Neither satisfied nor dissatisfied
(d) Dissatisfied
(e) Very dissatisfied
(f) Don't know

Q50. Do you need support or advice on equal opportunities issues but do not know how to get it?
(a) Yes
(b) No

BUILDING INVOLVEMENT

This section is about the way in which your group involves people, and relates with other groups and agencies.

Q51. Please indicate below the ways in which your group is accountable to your community and/or users: (*please circle any that apply*)
(a) Annual election of representatives
(b) Newsletters
(c) Regular feedback meetings
(d) Other (*please describe*)_____

Q52. What approaches does the group use to find out the needs of the local community and/or users: (*please circle any that apply*)
(a) Consultation meetings
(b) Outreach work
(c) Questionnaires
(d) Other (*please describe*)_____

Q53. Has the group been involved in joint work over the last year with any of the following? (e.g. jointly running a campaign/festival/play-scheme/organisation or training or new projects etc. (*If yes, please circle any that apply*)
(a) With the Council
(b) With other statutory agencies (eg health authority)
(c) Other (*please specify*)_____

Q54. Is the group a member of any formal networks?
(a) Yes   *Please go to Question 55*
(b) No   *Please go to Question 60*

Q55. Please list the formal networks that your group belongs to.

Q56. Of those networks listed, which one is most benefit to your work in the area?

Q57. Please indicate how effective the network is in carrying out the following roles.
(*Please circle one number for each role on a scale of 1 to 10, where 1 = Not effective at all and 10 = Highly effective*)

(a) Exchange of information	1 2 3 4 5 6 7 8 9 10
(b) Co-ordination of activities in the area	1 2 3 4 5 6 7 8 9 10
(c) Exchange of skills and learning	1 2 3 4 5 6 7 8 9 10
(d) Giving support and confidence	1 2 3 4 5 6 7 8 9 10
(e) Representing members in consultation/partnership	1 2 3 4 5 6 7 8 9 10
(f) Developing a sense of common purpose	1 2 3 4 5 6 7 8 9 10

Q58. Please describe any other roles that you think the networks should have to support the work of your group.

Q59. Please describe any barriers to your group's fuller participation in this network.

Q60. How are you supported in getting involved in links with other community groups?

Q61. Please give the names and addresses of any other locally-based community groups that you know of.

Q62. Are there any general points or comments you would like to make?

Further help

☐ An electronic copy of the questions checklists in Resources One and Two is available free in rich text format (RTF) for readers of *Assessing Community Strengths*. It means you will not need to retype the questions. Email: **cogs@cogs.solis.co.uk**

☐ In addition, a module containing the community strengths questions has been developed for COMPASS users. (COMPASS is a community profiling software package. See Resource Eight, p. 156 below)

Resource Two: The Support Organisations Survey Questions

This survey is for collecting information on the level of support in the area.

Introduction

Below are listed questions that you can use in designing your questionnaire for the survey of community and voluntary groups in your area. In using this list and designing your questionnaire please bear in mind the following points:

- Do not use all the questions as you will end up with a questionnaire form that is far too long. Use the list to decide which mix of questions suit your needs.

- Again several question options will need either circling (which we have used here) or tick boxes which look like this: ☐

- Several questions refer to the 'area'. The use of the questions in a survey will consequently need a covering letter or guidelines for people completing the form on what the area covers.

- It is advisable to include with your questionnaire a clear description of what the term 'support' means, otherwise you will receive a variety of vague responses to your questions! Information on defining support is also given in Part Three, p. 38.

Checklist of questions on level of support

Q1. **Name of your organisation.**

Q2. **Address, telephone number and email address.**

Q3. **Contact name and job title (and address if different from above).**

Q4. **Please describe briefly, in the space below, the main aims and activities of the organisation:**

      Aims: _____

   Activities: _____

If you have a description of your aims and objectives please include a copy with this completed form.

Q5. **Please describe the area you cover:** (*please circle one*)
    (a) Whole district   *Please go to Question 7*
    (b) The area   *Please go to Question 8*
    (c) Immediate neighbourhood.   *Please go to Question 6*

Q6. **If immediate neighbourhood only, please describe where in terms of main streets.**

Q7. **If whole district, please say what proportion of your activities/services are provided only in the area.**

Q8. **Please describe the type of community and voluntary groups your organisation supports, for example tenants' associations.** *The term 'group' means an actual body of people who meet together to carry out activities or provide services – it does not mean in this instance just the type of person, such as lone parents.*

Q9. **If you work with minority ethnic groups, please say which ones.**

Q10. How long has your organisation been working in the area?

BUILDING SKILLS

This section is about the ways in which organisations help to build the skills, knowledge and confidence of people involved in local community and voluntary groups. It concerns training and learning activities that are specifically designed for people to contribute to and lead community and voluntary groups.

How training is organised

Q11. Do you directly provide or organise course-based training for community groups and voluntary groups (*please circle*)?

(a) Yes   (b) No

If yes please give a general description of this training over the last two years, including brief information on title of course, accreditation, location, etc.

Course title	Provide	Organiser	Accredited?	Location	Comments

Q12. Do you provide or organise tailor-made training for community and voluntary groups, e.g. training sessions designed particularly for one community group?

(a) Yes   (b) No

If yes, please describe any which have been run during the last two years.

Q13. **Please indicate which of the following areas are covered in training your organisation provides** (*please circle any that apply*):

(a) Publicity: producing newsletters, leaflets, posters

(b) The media: press releases, getting on with the media

(c) Money: bookkeeping, accounts

(d) Presentation skills

(e) Computer skills, e.g. word processing

(f) Managing staff

(g) Managing a building

(h) Equal opportunities

(i) Fundraising

(j) Planning the group's/organisation's activities

(k) Community work skills

(l) Evaluation

(m) Working as a team/resolving conflicts

(n) Working in partnerships

(o) Working with the Council

(p) Working with projects and agencies

(q) Others (*please list*)_____

Q14. **Do you support the development of skills of community and voluntary groups through any other kinds of activity?** (*please circle any that apply*):

(a) Mentoring schemes for members of community groups

(b) Sharing skills through joint working

(c) Running a resource library

(d) Organising visits or exchanges

(e) Secondments to groups

(f) Learning from experience/action

(g) Others (*please describe*)_____

Q15. **Can you help community and voluntary groups to identify their training needs?**

(a) Yes   (b) No

If yes please describe _____

Q16. **Do you provide training resources and support that community and voluntary groups can use to run their own training?**

(a) Yes   (b) No

If yes, which of the following? (*please circle any that apply*)

(a) Childcare

(b) Grants

(c) Rooms

(d) Training materials, e.g. flipcharts

(e) Administration of courses

(f) Developing new courses

(g) Guidance for participants

(h) Advice on funding

(i) Other (*please specify*)_____

Advice

Q17. **Does your organisation provide advice, either formally or informally, to community and voluntary groups on any of the following?** (*please circle any that apply*)
(a) Using the media
(b) Managing projects
(c) Meetings and committee skills
(d) Developing the organisation
(e) Planning
(f) Funding
(g) Finances and bookkeeping
(h) Team building
(i) Others (*please specify*) _____

BUILDING ORGANISATIONS

This section is about ways that organisations help to build community and voluntary groups, developing their strength and organisational capacity.

Money

Q18. **Does your organisation provide funding/grant aid for community and voluntary groups in this area?** (*please circle*)

(a) Yes   (b) No

If yes, please include with the completed form, information on the criteria for grant aid to groups.

Practical resources

Q19. **Do you have any practical equipment or resources community and voluntary groups can access and use?** (*Please indicate if a charge is made by ticking the appropriate box for each resource.*)

Resource/facility	Free	Charge
Use of telephone		
Fax facilities		
Desk space		
Photocopying facilities		
Use of a computer		
Access to the Internet		
Meeting space		
Storage space		
Kitchen		
Transport		
Administrative support		
Other (*please specify*)		

Q20. Any conditions or comments on use.

Q21. Are there any restrictions in terms of the types of community and voluntary groups that can use these resources? (*please circle*)

(a) Yes   (b) No

If yes, please describe _____

Q22. Are you happy for the information in your response to the last two questions to be made available to community and voluntary groups? (*please circle*)

(a) Yes   (b) No

Community work

Q23. How many paid community workers does your organisation employ that spend time working with community groups in this area?

(a) Full-time _____ (b) Part-time _____

Q24. Please describe their roles:

BUILDING EQUALITY

This section looks at ways in which larger organisations and agencies help to build equality within community and voluntary groups and the communities within which they work.

Q25. Do you support community and voluntary groups in developing their own equal opportunities initiatives in any of the following ways? (*please circle any that apply*)

(a) Help writing equal opportunities policies/statements
(b) Providing training, e.g. on cultural awareness
(c) Advice on equal opportunities practice, e.g., recruitment
(d) Funding for equal opportunities initiatives, e.g., increased access
(e) Provision of translators/interpreters
(f) Awareness raising
(g) Running campaigns, e.g. anti-racism campaigns
(h) Other (*please describe*)_____

Q26. Are there any other ways your organisation is working with community and voluntary groups to promote and implement equal opportunities?

If yes, please describe _____

BUILDING INVOLVEMENT

This section concerns ways organisations help to build the capacity of community and voluntary groups to involve people and contribute to local decision-making.

Q27. **Please indicate in which of the following ways you support community and voluntary groups to:** (*please circle any that apply*)
(a) Be accountable to their own community/users
(b) Find out about the needs of the local community/users
(c) Work jointly with other community and voluntary organisations
(d) Work jointly with the Council
(e) Work jointly with statutory agencies
(f) Form and run networks

Q28. **Please describe the help you give community and voluntary groups to take action, for example to set up and run their own projects/campaigns/services?**

Q29. **Which of the following do you help community and voluntary groups to have a say in:** (*please circle any that apply*)
(a) Developing local projects
(b) Delivery of local services
(c) Regeneration programmes
(d) Policies of the Council and other statutory agencies e.g., health authority
(e) Other (*please specify*)_____

Q30. **Please describe the nature of this help.**

Q31. **Does your organisation have a policy on any of the following** (*please circle any that apply*)**:**
(a) Equal opportunities
(b) Consulting and involving local people
(c) Community development

If yes to any, please include a copy of each policy with this completed form.

Q32. **Please describe any other ways in which your organisation supports and builds the strength of community and voluntary groups.**

LINKS

The section looks at the links your organisation has with other organisations in the area.

Q33. **Are you involved in any networks of organisations that are active in the area whose members provide support for community and voluntary groups.**
If yes, please describe:_____

Q34. Do you jointly plan your support for voluntary and community groups with any other organisation?
If yes, please describe:_____

LOOKING AHEAD

Finally it is very useful to know if for any of the areas of support described in this survey, your organisation has interest in increasing its contribution.

Q35. Please describe potential areas of growth in how your organisation could further support community and voluntary groups in future. (*Please refer to particular question numbers from this survey form above where appropriate.*)

Q36. What do you see as the main blocks to your organisation being able to increase its level of support for community and voluntary groups?

Q37. Can your organisation provide training and advice to other organisations, agencies or partnerships on community involvement? (*please circle*)
(a) Yes   (b) No

Q38. Please add any general comments/points you wish to contribute.

Resource Three: The Community Strengths Framework

Introducing the framework

The framework is designed to enable community and voluntary groups, large organisations and agencies to assess the area's community strengths, plan for action and build on these strengths. The aim of the framework is to provide a way to identify collectively what levels of community organisation and support exist in a specified area. The framework uses five levels and each of these is indicated by a series of characteristics, which relate to degrees of community organisation and support. It suggests that any one area is at a certain level for community organisation, and a certain level for support.

These levels have each been given a name to summarise each set of characteristics at that level:

Level 1: Creating
Level 2: Connecting
Level 3: Structuring
Level 4: Partnering
Level 5: Sustaining

The framework is also divided into categories based on the four key themes introduced earlier for use in the surveys: Building organisations, Building skills, Building equality, Building involvement. In combination, using both themes and levels can help to identify the overall pattern for a neighbourhood. By including the four themes, there is the scope to acknowledge that the area may be, for example, at Level One for Building skills but Level Three for Building organisations, and so on. In this way, it can be used to address these four different themes fairly directly. It can also address the same issues for the support organisations. They may be at different levels for different themes.

The framework therefore helps to measure the degree of community strengths, providing a baseline position against which future developments can be assessed.

The Community Strengths Framework

The levels of community organisation

BUILDING ORGANISATION

This is about the activity and development of community and voluntary groups and how they may work with other groups.

LEVEL 1 is indicated by ...	*Milestones*
✓ Groups show a low level of activity and organisation ✓ There is a low level of confidence and morale in community groups about the prospect of real change happening in their neighbourhood ✓ Not many people are playing a leadership role within their communities – it all falls on too few and they feel on their own! ✓ Groups identify several key issues as a significant problem in meeting their objectives ✓ Few groups have paid staff or high levels of volunteering ✓ Groups lack access to practical resources ✓ Groups lack access to the information they need to achieve their aims ✓ Few groups have access to community workers ✓ Groups are isolated from each other or from local networks	*Increase activity and involvement*

LEVEL 2 is indicated by ...	*Milestones*
✓ There are informal links between community and voluntary groups ✓ Involvement in community activity is increasing ✓ There is some knowledge of resources and support for community and voluntary groups ✓ Groups have reasonable access to practical resources	*Develop networks between groups*

Building organisation

LEVEL 3 is indicated by ...	*Milestones*
✓ There is an increasing range of community and voluntary groups ✓ Some networking activity between community and voluntary groups is established and there is a recognition of the value of joint planning and collaborative working ✓ There are effective links with local support organisations ✓ The level of planning of groups and involvement of members is reasonable ✓ There is a high level of turnout at management committee meetings ✓ Management committees show a broad balance of community representation ✓ The majority of groups have adequate and appropriate space/premises ✓ Several groups have an action plan ✓ A significant number of groups make use of outside advice ✓ A significant number of groups have access to information they need to achieve their aims	*Develop infrastructures which are locally accountable*

Building organisation

LEVEL 4 is indicated by ...	*Milestones*
✓ There are many and varied community and voluntary groups ✓ Joint working and links between groups are very effective ✓ Community and voluntary groups have representative bodies through which they can support each other and common issues can be progressed ✓ There is a real sense of achievement and pride in the community, enhanced by the apparent high level of community activity and project development ✓ There are local focal points for accessing information about community and voluntary groups ✓ Community and voluntary groups have a variety of sources of secure, ongoing income ✓ There are a variety of forms of constitutional status in place ✓ There is evidence of community enterprise and income generated from trading. ✓ There is a developing community asset base	*Develop active partnerships between community and voluntary groups, support agencies and relevant external bodies*

LEVEL 5 is indicated by ...	**Milestones**
✓ Groups are well motivated and have a strong sense of ownership and identity ✓ There is a highly organised community – effective support for groups is in place ✓ Active partnerships with external bodies are established ✓ Several groups have a well established asset base, i.e. own their own building or equipment ✓ Communities illustrate a high degree of confidence in creating change themselves ✓ Involvement in partnerships is based on principles of equality ✓ Community groups have access to the information they need to achieve their aims ✓ Community groups have sustainable funding	*Sustain community-led projects, partnerships and policies*

Building organisation

BUILDING SKILLS

This is about the ways in which groups can build the skills, knowledge and confidence of their members to enable them to be effective in achieving their aims and to fully participate in and benefit from regeneration and community development.

LEVEL 1 is indicated by:	*Milestones*
✓ There is little interest among groups in developing the skills of their members ✓ Very few groups participate in training or learning activities ✓ Locally available training is about skills for getting a job rather than designed for the needs of community groups	*Identify existing skills and training gaps*

LEVEL 2 is indicated by ...	*Milestones*
✓ There are some clear indications about the type of training groups need ✓ There is some awareness among community and voluntary groups of existing training provision ✓ Groups see access to training and learning as a problem ✓ There is some understanding of the skills and knowledge existing within groups but few opportunities for sharing them between groups. ✓ The groups feel the range of ways they can get involved in learning is very limited ✓ Most training that is available for groups is only accessed by local community leaders rather than the wider body of active members of groups	*Develop opportunities for sharing skills and knowledge*

Building skills

LEVEL 3 is indicated by ...	*Milestones*
✓ There are formal and informal opportunities to share knowledge, skills and experience between groups ✓ The training needs of groups in the area are effectively identified and acted on ✓ Support, training and learning opportunities for groups are well-organised and provided to a reasonable level ✓ Individuals in community and voluntary groups benefit from training and learning ✓ Opportunities are provided to have learning accredited ✓ There is clear evidence about what is stopping community and voluntary groups from making further use of learning and training opportunities ✓ Minority groups have access to training ✓ Agencies and local partnerships begin to address their training needs to work more effectively in communities	*Develop locally-relevant training courses and recognition for learning through action*

LEVEL 4 is indicated by ...	*Milestones*
✓ There is a range of flexible and accessible support, training and learning opportunities ✓ Networking, where community and voluntary groups benefit from exchange of information and ideas, is a key element of activity ✓ There are some examples of how involvement in community activity has helped people to access further training and employment ✓ Community and voluntary groups are recognised for, and feel confident in, bringing and sharing significant skills to the regeneration/development process ✓ Community members possess the skills to effectively manage an increasing range of community-led projects ✓ Access to training by minority groups is effectively and systematically addressed	*Analyse the existing relationship between skills development and community strengths – plan for the future with local partners*

Building skills

LEVEL 5 is indicated by ...	*Milestones*
✓ Community and voluntary groups regularly identify their own training needs and are supported in meeting them ✓ There is an increasing range of successful community-led projects ✓ Communities are sufficiently skilled to manage strategies and develop partnerships ✓ Minority groups participate effectively in available training and learning opportunities ✓ Communities are contributing effectively to local and regional strategic development	*Ensure continual access to learning opportunities*

Building skills

BUILDING EQUALITY

Building equality is about the ways in which community and voluntary groups are inclusive and the extent to which community and voluntary groups try to help to build equality within their group and in communities.

LEVEL 1 is indicated by:	*Milestones*
✓ Very few groups have an equal opportunities policy ✓ Very few groups are promoting equality and access ✓ There is little awareness and knowledge about different community needs and perspectives ✓ There is little evidence of community and voluntary groups taking action to challenge discrimination	*Increase knowledge and awareness of community diversity*

LEVEL 2 is indicated by ...	*Milestones*
✓ There is some recognition and awareness of different interests and perspectives within the community ✓ Some community and voluntary groups have developed their own equal opportunities policies ✓ There is an awareness that 'open to all' statements may be meaningless unless action is taken to encourage and support people's involvement ✓ Some groups can be seen to be implementing their equal opportunities policies in order to broaden involvement and maximise benefit ✓ Groups are identifying additional resources they require to enhance people's involvement ✓ There is an increasing take-up of training and awareness opportunities by groups around equalities issues	*Share best practice*

Building equality

LEVEL 3 is indicated by ...	*Milestones*
✓ Groups are increasingly aware of the ways they can unconsciously discriminate against potential members and users ✓ Some solutions to address barriers are developed through raised awareness and community collaboration ✓ An increasing number of community and voluntary groups have equal opportunities action plans ✓ Groups are accessing resources to enhance equality ✓ Groups are challenging other groups and agencies around inclusion issues ✓ New groups are forming to meet previously unmet need ✓ An increasing range of groups feel involved and that their needs are being met ✓ Networks are inclusive of a variety of local interests and perspectives, as appropriate to their aims	*Target under-represented groups and promote access and inclusion*

LEVEL 4 is indicated by ...	*Milestones*
✓ There are integrated strategies for increased access and involvement across a range of community and voluntary groups and agencies ✓ An increasing range of groups feel involved and contribute to the development of their communities ✓ Groups' activities include a diverse range of people and interests ✓ Groups can provide evidence of how they are effectively open to all ✓ Community leaders reflect the diversity of the communities and areas they represent ✓ Several groups have effective equal opportunities monitoring systems	*Develop strategic action to ensure all community members benefit from activities*

Building equality

LEVEL 5 is indicated by ...	Milestones
✓ The area has a diverse range of active community groups that reflect the rich diversity of cultures ✓ The majority of groups in the area are actively implementing equal opportunities policies and reviewing their practice ✓ Groups are effectively learning from others' good practice ✓ A broad range of interest groups are actively involved in strategic development and planning processes	*Regularly review and address barriers to involvement*

Building equality

BUILDING INVOLVEMENT

This is about the extent community and voluntary groups involve people and contribute to and influence local decision-making.

LEVEL 1 is indicated by:	Milestones
✓ Only a few people participate in community and voluntary groups ✓ Groups are isolated with few opportunities for networking ✓ Very few groups have a say in local decision-making ✓ Groups rarely find out about the needs of their local community or their service users ✓ There arc inadequate methods of passing on information about activities and other opportunities for involvement	*Bring groups together and share strengths*

LEVEL 2 is indicated by ...	*Milestones*
✓ There are some consultation processes in place ✓ Some groups have a say in local decision-making ✓ Some groups find out about needs by consulting their members and users ✓ There are some networks through which groups can meet and share concerns, ideas and solutions ✓ There are limited opportunities for groups to effectively represent their constituencies	*Publicise existing consultation/ networking mechanisms and develop new ones as appropriate*

Building involvement

LEVEL 3 is indicated by ...	*Milestones*
✓ Community and voluntary groups reflect the needs of their membership ✓ Community and voluntary groups have significant levels of active membership ✓ There is a broad range of people advocating/representing their groups and the interests of members ✓ A wide range of community and voluntary groups share commitment and motivation to bring about change and development in their communities ✓ There are established links between community and voluntary groups and external agencies ✓ Consultation mechanisms are effectively used by groups ✓ Groups feel encouraged and supported to have a say in decision-making ✓ An increasing number and range of groups are informed about local plans and are able to make informed contributions to development opportunities	*Develop accountable and representative structures*

LEVEL 4 is indicated by ...	*Milestones*
✓ There is effective support for groups to take action ✓ Several key groups in the area implement community involvement policies ✓ There is a 'healthy' turnover of group leaders and representatives ✓ Most groups systematically find out the needs of their communities and have effective information channels ✓ The majority of groups have 'transparent' and accessible operating policies and procedures ✓ Local people are involved in managing local projects	*Implement community participation strategies across all sectors*

Building involvement

LEVEL 5 is indicated by …	*Milestones*
✓ Community and voluntary groups are engaged in developmental activity with partners from a range of sectors ✓ Local resources are increasingly controlled by local people involved in groups and networks ✓ Groups and networks have recognised and effective roles in local decision-making and strategic planning of agencies and partnerships ✓ Consultation and participation is planned with groups to avoid unco-ordinated and over-demanding activities.	*Provide continuing support for community-led developments*

Building involvement

The Community Strengths Framework

The levels of support

BUILDING ORGANISATIONS

This is about ways that support organisations help to build community and voluntary groups, developing their strength and organisational capacity.

LEVEL 1 is indicated by:	*Milestones*
✓ There is little developmental support for community groups from larger support organisations and agencies ✓ Funding for groups is very limited and short term ✓ There are few organisations providing practical help to groups with resources, space or equipment ✓ Information on what support is available is hard to obtain	*Identify the immediate needs of groups and the potential support available*

LEVEL 2 is indicated by ...	*Milestones*
✓ Organisations are beginning to look at the resource needs of local groups ✓ Some organisations provide access to practical resources but it is unco-ordinated and unpublicised ✓ Some funding is available to community and voluntary groups but only on a short-term basis ✓ There are some community workers in the neighbourhood but their roles are unclear	*Bring organisations and groups together to share information*

LEVEL 3 is indicated by ...	*Milestones*
✓ Funding to groups is available and reasonably well publicised ✓ Organisations are aware of the resources required by groups and are working to help meet these needs ✓ There are several community workers who are networking and trying to work strategically ✓ There is reasonable access for groups to practical resources	*Develop a network to plan and co-ordinate support and resources*

Building organisations

LEVEL 4 is indicated by ...	*Milestones*
✓ Access to practical resources is co-ordinated and well publicised ✓ Groups can access advice to develop organisationally which is free and well publicised ✓ Community work in the area is co-ordinated between the organisations providing it	*Build a strategic partnership between organisations and groups to ensure a 'match' of needs and support*

LEVEL 5 is indicated by ...	*Milestones*
✓ Organisations have a locally agreed strategy on the support they provide to groups in terms of advice, resources and funding ✓ The provision of advice, funding and resources is based on a systematic assessment of needs question ✓ Provision for community groups is well publicised ✓ Community work is well resourced and co-ordinated and evaluated by both providers and local groups	*Maintain processes for assessing need and support to reflect change*

Building organisations

BUILDING SKILLS

This is about the ways in which organisations help to build the skills, knowledge and confidence of people involved in local community and voluntary groups. It concerns training and learning activities that are specifically designed for people to contribute to and lead community and voluntary groups. It is also about the skills and abilities of people working for and involved in local partnerships and support organisations.

LEVEL 1 is indicated by …	*Milestones*
✓ There are few opportunities for groups to participate in training and learning to increase their effectiveness as groups ✓ Existing provision is not based on identified local needs and is rather formal in style ✓ The range and content of training available for groups is very limited ✓ Support agencies show little awareness of the need to improve their abilities to work effectively with community and voluntary groups	*Identify content and style of training required*

LEVEL 2 is indicated by …	*Milestones*
✓ The range of ways groups can get involved in learning is limited ✓ Some organisations provide training for local community groups though it is still rather limited and inflexible in content and style ✓ Support agencies and local partnerships begin to address their training needs to work more effectively in communities	*Develop a training needs strategy with group*

Building skills

LEVEL 3 is indicated by ...	*Milestones*
✓ Organisations provide a reasonable range of training and learning opportunities ✓ Training and learning provision is based on consideration of local needs ✓ Some training is tailor-made for particular groups ✓ Organisations offer some further support to groups organising their own training exploring a wider range of activities to support local learning ✓ Some organisations can help local groups to identify their training needs ✓ Groups can get advice on funding and organisational issues ✓ Organisations are involved in looking at their own learning and training needs to increase their ability to work effectively with local groups	*A wide range of training opportunities meeting a wide range of needs*

LEVEL 4 is indicated by ...	*Milestones*
✓ Training and learning opportunities for local groups is systematically based on needs and well publicised question ✓ Organisations regularly provide training and learning opportunities for their own staff to increase their ability to work effectively with local groups ✓ Organisations provide a range of activities to support learning in local groups such as mentoring, resource libraries and secondments ✓ Advice for groups on funding and management issues is well organised	*Analyse the existing relationship between skills development and community strengths – plan for the future with local partners*

Building skills

LEVEL 5 is indicated by ...	*Milestones*
✓ Training and learning opportunities for groups are well resourced and integrated into mainstream budgets of support organisations ✓ Support agencies and local partnerships systematically address their own training and learning needs to work more effectively in communities ✓ Organisations work jointly with local groups to plan advice, training and learning opportunities ✓ Organisations learn from the experience of other organisations and from community groups ✓ Organisations provide a range of creative activities to support learning in local groups such as mentoring, resource libraries and secondments ✓ Training and learning is enjoyable!	*Ensure continual access to learning opportunities for agencies and groups*

Building skills

BUILDING EQUALITY

This is about ways in which larger organisations and agencies help to build equality within community and voluntary groups and the communities within which they work.

LEVEL 1 is indicated by:	*Milestones*
✓ Few organisations actively promote equality in their support of local groups ✓ Very few organisations have an equal opportunities policy ✓ There is little awareness and knowledge about different community needs and perspectives ✓ There is little evidence of organisations taking action to challenge discrimination	*Increase knowledge and awareness of community diversity*

LEVEL 2 is indicated by ...	*Milestones*
✓ Some organisations have equal opportunities policies and are implementing them ✓ Some organisations are actively challenging discrimination in the practice and provision ✓ There is some recognition and awareness of different interests and perspectives	*Share examples of good practice*

LEVEL 3 is indicated by ...	*Milestones*
✓ Organisations are developing equal opportunities such as training on cultural awareness ✓ Organisations are actively involved in challenging discrimination ✓ Some organisations are actively funding local equal opportunities initiatives such as increased access to buildings ✓ Information on the needs of marginalised groups is sensitively collected and acted upon	*Issues around access and inclusion are high profile*

Building equality

LEVEL 4 is indicated by ...	*Milestones*
✓ Organisations are working jointly with local groups to challenge discrimination ✓ Funding and support provided by many organisations encourages local groups to develop and promote equality ✓ Many organisations have equal opportunities policies and are implementing them ✓ Many organisations run training on cultural awareness for their staff	*An equalities strategy is 'owned' by organisations and groups*

LEVEL 5 is indicated by ...	*Milestones*
✓ Groups and organisations work jointly on activities to promote equal opportunities and challenge discrimination ✓ Organisations provide a wide range of activities to support equal opportunities initiatives carried out by groups ✓ The majority of organisations implement equal opportunities policies	*Regularly review and address barriers to involvement*

Building equality

BUILDING INVOLVEMENT

**This is about ways organisations
help to build the capacity of community
and voluntary groups to involve people
and contribute to local decision-making.**

LEVEL 1 is indicated by ...	*Milestones*
✓ Very few organisations give local groups a say in how services are organised ✓ There is a lack of information on support that organisations provide ✓ Organisations rarely find out about local needs ✓ There are few examples of joint working between community groups and organisations in the area ✓ Networks do not involve community groups	*Bring organisations and groups together and identify the benefits of involvement*

LEVEL 2 is indicated by ...	*Milestones*
✓ Some organisations consult local groups on decisions about support and services ✓ Organisations are beginning to find out about the local needs ✓ There is a limited amount of information available about local agencies and activities	*Publicise existing partnerships and develop new networks as appropriate*

LEVEL 3 is indicated by ...	*Milestones*
✓ Networks are open to community groups and use this information to plan support for community groups ✓ Organisations regularly consult groups and use this information to plan their support question ✓ There are regular and effective consultation mechanisms in place ✓ Organisations are beginning to use a range of ways to consult and involve community groups ✓ There are a variety of information strategies in place to share information about what is going on in the area	*Develop engaging processes as well as accountable and representative structures*

Building involvement

LEVEL 4 is indicated by ...	*Milestones*
✓ Several key organisations implement community involvement policies ✓ Networks are proactive in involving community groups ✓ Local partnerships encourage and actively support the involvement of community groups through appropriate networks ✓ Support for community groups is based on consultation and joint planning ✓ Blocks that prevent organisations providing effective support are identified	*Implement community participation strategies across all sectors*

LEVEL 5 is indicated by ...	*Milestones*
✓ Networks and partnerships are well organised and effectively involve local community groups ✓ Support for community groups is based on a jointly planned strategy, reflecting local needs and agreed priorities ✓ The local partnerships actively lead on involving local groups in decision-making on services in the area ✓ Blocks that prevent organisations providing effective support are tackled and overcome	*Provide continuing support for community-led developments*

Building involvement

Resource Four: Action Points

Once a baseline position has been established using the framework, it is likely that community groups and support agencies will want to identify what they can do next to help move the area up from its existing levels.

The Framework identifies some possible action in very general terms. The following pages provide some much more specific examples of potential activities. These are intended to help and prompt discussion during the workshop and focus groups as well as inform the writing of the action report. They are not the only or necessarily the most appropriate steps to take. This will depend on local circumstances and context as well as consideration and recognition of an ever-changing political environment.

The action points can be used to create a plan of development over time that can help to co-ordinate the activities of groups, community workers, agencies and other key organisations. This will obviously need to be an open process and one which is evaluated after a certain period of time to ensure it responds to current needs.

BUILDING ORGANISATIONS

Some considerations

☐ What are the circumstances in which community groups develop and flourish?

☐ Do networks encompass and reflect the range of interests promoted through community groups in the area?

☐ How are support organisations enabling community groups to manage themselves effectively?

Examples of action

- Bring together all the community and voluntary groups identified in the survey to share ideas for circulating the information gathered, to analyse the particular difficulties they face, to identify potential support and ways in which they might usefully work together.

- Identify and make contact with potential support providers within the community. Encourage them to respond to your profile findings.

- Publicise the survey information and any suggested developments to raise awareness of what is going on, e.g. through a local newsletter, on tape, in the local paper's community column, in libraries, on public noticeboards.

- Organise events for all the community that provide an opportunity for people to get to know what's going on and find out about events organised by others and take along information about community and voluntary groups.

- Support newly emerging organisations with advice, practical resources, links to other organisations.

- Identify gaps in community group activity – are there sections of the community who have little opportunity for involvement and are there community and voluntary groups who are not part of the developing network? Make contact with them to explore what might be stopping them from participating and what can be done to aid their involvement.

- Explore how organisations and the wider community can benefit from some collaboration. You could start by finding ways of sharing resources and supporting each other, e.g. shared publicity, use of computers etc.

- Continue to widen the extent and range of community participation, both in community and voluntary groups and in networks.

- Formalise the networking that is taking place. Develop collective ownership of, and responsibility for, representative bodies such as community forums. This body should reflect a wide range of interests and perspectives. Agree the purpose, structure, accountability mechanisms and appropriate status of this body.

- Develop working relationships with external bodies and potential long-term partners.

- Actively participate in networks and structures that cut across community boundaries and operate across larger geographical and interest areas.

- Develop a long-term strategy for maintaining community and voluntary groups and activity.

- Support community and voluntary organisations to be autonomous and self sustaining.

- Build organisational capacity for the future – assess community structures and management models to ensure they are sustainable, i.e. how are the people moving on being replaced, is there financial stability?

- Take a strategic approach to development – establish partnerships with a range of relevant stakeholders.

- Be proactive in forming new partnerships for as long as necessary.

- Ensure that there is ongoing accountability to communities and that all community needs are recognised and reflected in development plans.

- Use your knowledge and experience to support less well-developed groups to build their capacity.

- Review effectiveness of organisational support.

- Promote positive experience to create a climate in which the voluntary and community sectors are respected as the lead body on relevant agendas.

BUILDING SKILLS

Some considerations

☐ Is there support for community groups to access training courses, e.g. are they run locally, at appropriate times, are expenses paid, is it in relevant languages?

☐ Are there opportunities for informal learning and in what ways is this learning recognised?

• How are support organisations identifying and acting upon their learning needs?

Examples of action

• Check if any other organisations have carried out a skills audit and/or training needs survey in the community (e.g., the Council's Education Department, the TEC/Learning and Skills Council, the Employment Service). Are they planning to act upon this information?

• Bring together community and voluntary groups to identify existing skills and their future training needs. Explore ways in which they might support each other.

• Turn your survey information into a directory of local training provision (and where and when it takes place, etc) and skills that are locally available. Circulate this as widely as possible.

• Hold a workshop for community members to explore their perceptions about skills development and the difficulties they face in accessing training.

• Organise some events, e.g. community lunches and networking fairs, to encourage and enable community and voluntary groups to share and develop their skills and knowledge.

• Look at the needs of groups to participate in the demands of running local projects, not just their own groups.

• Talk to training providers and local development agencies about their potential input and support in the development of new opportunities.

• Try to find solutions to some of the barriers to participation in community-based learning opportunities, e.g. develop informal routes to participation and take-up such as parent and toddler groups and 'drop-ins', and explore the extent of support and 'access' such as child and dependant care, bilingual support, use of accessible venues.

• Look at the needs of groups to participate in the demands of running the regeneration programme, not just projects or their own groups.

• Build involvement of members of groups in training, not just leaders.

• Negotiate and organise the provision of new training opportunities that support community activity, involvement and development.

• Explore methods of formally recognising people's involvement in community activity and training through accreditation arrangements, e.g. through Open College Network.

• Begin to evaluate the impact of skills development on community activity and vice versa.

- Proactively target organisations identified as less involved in community activity and development and review who is and isn't accessing training opportunities.

- Analyse how skills developed so far will further community development and identify any additional skills required.

- Use existing networks within and between communities and agencies to develop strategic partnerships which will enhance the building of skills.

- Explore the potential for communities to take on the provision of training previously provided by external agencies.

- Provide advice, training and support to other communities which may be at an earlier level of development.

- Ensure there is continuing access to learning opportunities and resources.

Building Equality

Some considerations

☐ Is there an awareness of different community interests and identities?

☐ Do groups and large organisations understand and implement equalities practice?

☐ How do groups and large organisations share resources to promote greater access and involvement?

Examples of action

- Encourage organisations to share good practice around promoting equality.

- Organisations should involve their members in exploring whether their services are reaching all the people they should be – consider different ethnic groups, different cultural groups, men and women, different age groups (e.g, children, older people), lesbians, gay men, people with disabilities.

- Collect information on the make-up of the local area and make this publicly available in appropriate languages and a variety of forms.

- Identify what helps and what stops people being active in groups.

- Share information about where to get help re equal opportunities and support resources such as signers, translators, interpreters, etc.

- Encourage and support the translation of public information into relevant community languages.

- Identify, and provide for, training needs around anti-discriminatory practice and equal opportunities action plans.

- Share good practice between groups.

- Establish funding channels for equal opportunities initiatives and support resources.

- Organise events that appreciate different local interests and cultures.

- Use a range of techniques and styles to allow as many people as possible to get involved – hold meetings but also informal gatherings, visual exercises, etc., if people aren't coming to events, go to them – in the pub, in the mosque, in the school, in the youth club, etc.

- Wherever possible, provide for the costs of child and dependant care.

- Profile community diversity and promote positive images of community members.

- Develop and implement action plans with relevant targets around the full involvement of black and minority ethnic communities in area initiatives. Monitor expenditure of local programme initiatives (e.g., regeneration, health and education) on marginalised groups, and feed into future programmes.

- Bring equality/positive action services into mainstream expenditure.

BUILDING INVOLVEMENT

Some considerations

☐ Are there a variety of ways in which groups can have a say such as events other than public meetings?

☐ What are the processes by which community groups are made aware of, and are assisted to understand, structures and procedures?

☐ Are agencies implementing community participation strategies?

Examples of action

- Using the profile information, publicise what's going on and circulate widely.

- Build on current strengths – don't ignore them!

- Bring organisations and agencies together to discuss further opportunities for participation.

- Identify opportunities for some 'quick wins'.

- Develop a budget to support people's involvement, e.g. to cover travel costs, telephone calls, postage, photocopying, etc.

- Organise a community festival to bring people together and raise awareness of activities and issues.

- Carry out a skills audit to gain knowledge about what people have to offer and the training that might be needed.

- Find ways of valuing and appreciating people's voluntary contributions, through naming them in an annual report, holding an annual 'awards ceremony', holding a party, etc.

- Always try to ensure that meetings and events are held at times and places which are appropriate, e.g. in accessible venues with accessible toilets, on bus routes, in well-lit and familiar areas, not at tea time, etc.

- Use existing networks and contacts with community leaders and local paid workers to build involvement and strength.

- Develop an information strategy which includes a mixture of using local newsletters, local media (radio/television/newspapers), a leafleting campaign, a word-of-mouth approach

- Provide explanation and support so that everyone is able to have their say from an informed viewpoint, perhaps through insisting on plain language, induction sessions or pre meetings, developing a 'jargon buster' and so on.

- Ensure any procedures around money, policy development, recruitment and election are understandable and open to scrutiny.

- Review procedures with a view to simplification and be on the look out for unnecessary bureaucracy – it is often restrictive without having a useful purpose.

- Consider and plan for the realistic time-scales that will be needed for people to get involved and the notice periods many groups will require (e.g. many community groups only meet once a month and so the turnaround of information may be six weeks).

- Welcome challenge and be prepared to discuss concerns and issues – it is often the start of involvement.

- Try to organise fun activities, and celebrate successes.

- Establish mechanisms for mentoring and 'shadowing' so that new people can learn the ropes and develop skills to take on roles in the future.

- Develop creative and culturally sensitive forms of participation which provide different routes 'in' to having a say.

- Work with agencies to develop community involvement policies and strategies.

Resource Five: Running the Workshop

The main elements of the workshop are described in Part Five, p.63 above. Here we go into the aims of the workshop in more detail as well as describe the different methods that can be used.

The workshop forms a key part of the process of assessing community strengths. This section will help you to plan your own workshop and covers:

- aims

- format

- exercises

- action points.

Aims

The aims of the workshop can be to:

- give feedback to all those who have contributed to the surveys, including an initial analysis of all the information gathered

- clarify any ambiguous information contained in the findings

- provide participants with an opportunity to work collectively towards consensual understanding if conflicting information and perspectives have arisen through the survey process

- gather additional information about an area – particularly that which would be difficult to capture on a survey form such as the levels of morale amongst community organisations and their confidence in achieving change

- develop collective agreement about the current level of organisation and level of support

- identify action to further develop skills, organisations, equality and involvement

- provide a networking opportunity.

Once the initial findings from the community profile have been presented and discussed, the workshop can be used to gather and share additional information. Collecting additional information is important as there may be some areas that have not been covered by the surveys. This may be because of the need to keep the survey forms to a limited size, it may be that there are evident gaps in the information collected or there may be information that is hard to capture through a paper questionnaire. For example, information about how groups and agencies link together, and share information and skills might best be gathered through a collective exercise which itself promotes networking. Equally, assessing levels of morale, optimism and confidence can be carried out reasonably quickly through a participative exercise.

The key part of the workshop – not to be missed – is the exercise on stocktaking. This creates the opportunity for participants, who ideally represent a good cross-section of local groups and support organisations, to agree collectively on the level of community organisation for their area. This participative approach to deciding on the level is a central feature of community strengths assessments, ensuring a sense of ownership and involvement.

Format

Here is a suggested format or programme for the workshop – you will need a minimum of three hours to cover everything. Examples of exercises and tools to carry it out are described below.

- Welcome and introductions
- Outline aims of workshop
- Feedback from the research
  (a) Short presentation
  (b) Invite questions on findings and discussion points
  (c) Break into small groups for more detailed discussion and comments on the findings. Groups could also be asked to identify any perceived gaps in the information
  (d) Feedback from small groups

Exercise One: Networks and networking

- What are the key formal/organised networks in the area?
- Which ones does your group/agency link with?
- Where are the more informal links that support your organisation?

Summarise and share information.

Exercise Two: Community morale

This involves assessing community morale in terms of levels of optimism and confidence about the potential for positive change in the area.

Summarise results.

Exercise Three: Taking stock

This involves identifying the baseline position through levels of development framework.

Exercise Four: Identify action points

- Break into four groups based on the four themes of building organisation, skills, equality and involvement.
- Feedback in whole group.

Close workshop ensuring everyone knows what will happen next.

General points about running the workshop

- Have copies of the draft findings available on the day. It is always worthwhile giving a verbal presentation of the key points on the findings. Participants can then be given the opportunity to ask questions, comment and identify any additional or different interpretations of the information.

- When presenting the findings, it makes sense to cluster them in the same way as the questions on the survey forms, using the four themes of Building organisation, Building skills, Building equality and Building involvement. This divides the information into bite-size chunks but also provides a manageable framework for considering the baseline position, current needs and potential future development.

Exercises

1. Networks and networking

Purpose: This exercise helps to share information about relevant networks, identify other ways in which groups and organisations might network, build stronger networks, create additional networks.

Resources: a set of children's big building blocks, for example Mega bricks, washable pens and a large space.

Process:
- Ask participants what are the key formal/organised networks in the area? Everyone shouts out the ones they know, very briefly describing their purpose. As they do so they write the name of the network onto a building block.

- Spread the blocks on the floor or on a large table.

- Ask participants which ones does your group/agency link with?
Everyone writes the name of their group or organisation onto a different coloured building block and attaches it to the appropriate network block. If there are several relevant networks, then ask participants to write the name of their group onto several blocks, one per block.

- Ask: Where are the more informal links that support their organisation?

- Ask if there are other ways in which your groups/organisations link with other groups/organisations, for example perhaps not through a network as such but by regularly meeting up with others at an area committee meeting or at the mosque etc. Again ask participants to write these onto building blocks (choose another colour) and place around the edge.

- Are there commonalties between the networks, e.g. do the same groups attend the same networks – if so is there a need for more than one?

- Are there ways in which the networks link together – can you join the sets of blocks in any way?

- Are there gaps – are there some groups/organisations present that are not part of any network. If so, are there some that might be appropriate, if not is there a need for an additional network, e.g. it might be the small community groups that aren't involved and they might want to form something specific to their needs.

Summarise the picture, and any agreed action points. Ensure that contact details/meeting times, etc of the networks identified are shared with the whole group.

Notes: This exercise is only introductory to assessing the role of networks. It may, however, usefully unearth certain patterns and problems that can be described in the action report and then form the basis of further work. See Resource Seven below.

2. Assessing community morale

Purpose: to 'measure' the morale of community groups.

Resources: flip chart paper and lots of pens.

Process:
- Write several positive statements onto flip chart paper with a gauge underneath.

    The statements aim to assess feelings of the participants, for example:
    'I am very hopeful that this area is changing for the better.'
    'My organisation feels it is making a difference.'
    'I feel that we are really going to play a part in influencing change.'

    The gauge could take the form of a 'percentameter' or a 'speedometer' with range intervals marked on it, for example:

    0   20   40   60   80   100

    ◇ Everyone is asked to tick the gauge where 0 is completely disagree and 100 is strongly agree. This will create a visual pattern of level of agreement for each statement.
    ◇ Everyone looks at the patterns, identifying collective agreement or disagreement. It might be useful to separate out community groups from larger organisations – perhaps with different colour pens.
    ◇ This exercise informs the next one.
    ◇ It is useful to repeat this exercise periodically to assess any change.

3. Taking stock

Purpose: to develop collectively a consensus about the level of community organisation in the area profiled.

Resources: To prepare for this exercise you will need to photocopy onto separate large sheets of paper all the different sections of the levels of community organisation, one to each page, printed in the Community Strengths Framework in Resource Three above. Each theme will consequently have six sheets – one for each level plus one that has the introductory description of the theme. The framework has been designed especially to allow easy photocopying in this way. Each corner of the workshop room will feature a theme each with the relevant six sheets pinned up. It will save time in the workshop itself by pinning these up beforehand. In photocopying each sheet ensure some room is left for people to be able to place their coloured stickers - some sheets may end up with 20 or more stickers on.

Here are examples of two posters on Building organisations copied from The Community Strengths Framework levels of community organisation.

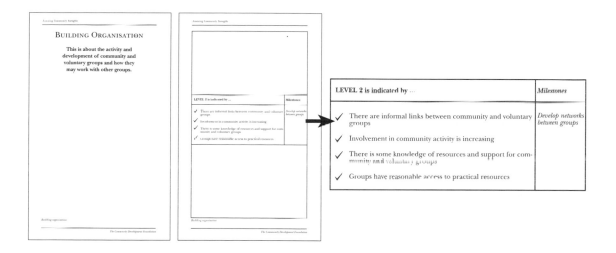

Process:
- The four themes and five levels are introduced and described briefly. A brief summary of the findings is given to remind participants of the main points.

- Give each participant four coloured stickers.

- Ask participants to look at each theme and stick a coloured dot on the level they think best describes their area having understood the findings and any subsequent analysis. This will involve a considerable amount of movement – and can be good fun! It helps if there is an accessible route around the room to get to the four corners easily.

- The next step is to ask every one to sit down and review the pattern of dots in each corner. The key question: is there a clear indication about the level of development for each theme? This will be reflected in the distribution of coloured dots. In many cases the pattern will stand out clearly with the majority of dots on one poster for each theme. If there is, or if there are roughly equal dots on two adjoining levels, move onto the next exercise. If not, the facilitator will need to stimulate some discussion to see if a consensus can be reached. This will involve identifying where there is common ground, and helping people to negotiate any points of disagreement. It may be useful to split the whole group into two groups, one for community groups and one for support organisations, to assess initially whether there is consensus within these groupings. This will be already apparent if the variation of the exercise described below has been used.

Variations and further development of the exercise:
- As indicated in Part 5 there are variations of this exercise depending on time and priorities. There may be differences in perception between small grass-roots groups and larger agencies which would be a useful issue to identify. This potential difference can be catered for by giving representatives of community groups and support organisations different colours of stickers to help identify any such differences in perception.

- A further development would be to also carry out the exercise of taking stock for the level of support as well as the level of community organisation. However the main reservation about this is that it may become too complicated. It requires each person having eight stickers and twice the number of sheets pinned on the walls for participants to read and think about. It depends partly on the amount of time the workshop can take. Doing it in two clearly defined stages would help. As suggested in Part Five, an easier alternative is for the workshop facilitators to present a view on the levels of support then open it for discussion and agreement.

Action points

Purpose: to collectively agree on short-term action and longer-term goals.

Resources: Action point suggestion lists (see Resource Four above); flip-chart paper.

Process:
- Ask participants to choose one of the four themes that is of particular interest to them.

- Break into groups based upon these preferences; give each group the relevant sheets from the walls for their information.

- Taking one theme per group, each group identifies areas for future activity which could help to take the neighbourhood to the next level. They may want to add additional characteristics to the sheets to give a more detailed and relevant description of the level for their area.

- Give the action point suggestions lists out at the start or nearer the end of the workshop depending on how much you think they will need prompting.

- Ask the groups to order their action points in terms of what can be done within the next three months, three to six months and six to twelve months.

- Bring all four groups together to share their ideas and identify who will take responsibility for the action points.

Resource Six: The Sandwell Case Study

Introduction

This approach was developed by the Community Development Foundation (CDF) on behalf of Sandwell Regeneration Partnership, as part of a research project across seven areas of Sandwell, West Midlands, in 1996 and 1997. A fuller description of this research, its findings and methodology is available in 'Neighbourhood Baselines for Capacity Building' by Peter Dale and Jayne Humm (2002).

In the Sandwell studies the research involved surveying the groups and community organisations as well as, in parallel, a statistical sample of households in those neighbourhoods. This enabled the researchers to see not only what was being done in terms of organised community activity, but what was *not* being done: how few, as well as how many, people were aware of the community organisations; whether they used them or were involved in them; also what stopped people getting involved and whether they would get more involved – or involved for the first time – if they had more opportunity. This provides key information for strategies to increase community activity and community capacity in local development.

The research methodology

The Sandwell research was based on the assumption that in order to assess existing local capacity, three things are needed:

- information about what local residents consider are the most important issues facing their community, and what they most wish to see available or remedied

- knowledge about existing community organisations, what they aim to achieve, and how strong they are

- the extent of local awareness of the work of these organisations, and how far local people are involved in them.

On the basis of this information, an assessment can be made of the extent to which local concerns are being addressed, and how effectively. This assessment in turn provides pointers to areas for future development, whether of new organisations to fill gaps in provision, or of existing organisations to strengthen responses.

It is almost certain, especially in a disadvantaged area, that many residents will *not* be active in the community. They may have been discouraged by a paucity of community and voluntary organisations, by an atmosphere of hopelessness or by feeling isolated through lack of work, money or amenities. Surveying the functioning community groups, therefore, whilst vitally important, will not indicate the level of activity amongst the majority of the population.

In the Sandwell research, the basic information was provided by two surveys, the household survey, and the community organisations survey.

The household survey

This comprised a sample survey of residents conducted by face-to-face interview in a randomly selected set of households. The two main purposes were to:

- identify what local residents saw as the main issues facing the area
- determine the level of awareness of community organisations in general and of particular organisations; to assess the level of involvement with this activity; and to identify the extent to which new groups might be supported.

Later versions also included questions about employment and training.

The community organisations survey

The second survey was a postal one, circulated to all community groups and organisations which could be identified within each area. It sought basic contact details, information about funding and organisational control, and information about who the organisation served and what it offered. Information about how much training and what resources were available was also requested. This survey provided details therefore about the extent and strength of the local community sector.

Combining the information from the two surveys enabled some judgements to be made about the relevance of current provision to local perceptions of need. The researchers were able to draw pointers for key areas of development, ways in which local organisations could be strengthened, and the most promising avenues for deploying the available development resources. The figures about community awareness and involvement, and the quality and quantity of community activity, provided numerical baselines against which progress could be measured in future years.

The approach developed in the Sandwell research is consequently an important complement to the approach described in assessing community strengths in the present publication. Broadly, the Sandwell studies provide a method to examine the level of community activity amongst a given population, whereas assessing community strengths – with its inclusion of the level of support and a five-level framework – is oriented more to measuring the capacity of community and voluntary organisations. This is a broad generalisation, however, and ideally, all three forms of survey would be combined – households, groups, and support organisations.

The policy background

During the 1980s, the increasing emphasis on ensuring that public sector programmes provided value for money led to the growing use of performance indicators – measures of the results of programmes and projects which could assess outcomes against previously defined targets. By the time of the introduction of the Single Regeneration Budget (SRB) in 1994, such use was widespread. SRB adopted a system whereby partnerships bidding for grants had to specify their intended outputs from a range of options covering such areas as housing, employment, education, health and amenities. Community involvement was initially encouraged and, in later rounds, required, but was not at first incorporated into the system of outputs. CDF used research evidence to propose that measurable outputs of community activity were possible, and needed to be incorporated into the SRB planning system alongside outputs on housing, jobs, etc. In the later rounds of SRB (and in a variety of other programmes such as some EU funding schemes) major steps were taken in this direction by the inclusion of 'capacity building' in the outputs. From 1998, capacity building and community involvement became a high priority, not only in the later rounds of SRB but also in other regeneration schemes such as the New Deal for Communities. A duty was placed on all local authorities in England and Wales from 2001 to establish a 'community strategy' linking all public services planning with a high degree of community involvement.

In the course of these developments, many local authorities, regeneration partnerships and community and voluntary umbrella groups began experimenting with ways of surveying the local community and voluntary sector in order to establish baselines and targets for developments. However, most such surveys registered only people who were already active in community and voluntary organisations. A comprehensive view of levels of activity and potential required some measure of informal activity and also methods of measuring inactivity: how many people in a given population were not active, not involved, not benefiting? It was only by establishing this picture that the significance of the level of existing activity could be seen, rather than assuming that it somehow represented or affected the whole local population. In fact, large sections of the population are often left untouched.

CDF's work

CDF had begun to address this issue of scale in the late 1980s and early 1990s. CDF played a major part in a study of active citizenship by the European Foundation for the Improvement of Living and Working Conditions (EFILWC – an EU body) which, for the first time, gave a comparative statistical and analytical picture of community organisations in case-study localities in seven EU countries (Chanan, 1992). In addition, CDF looked at one of its own larger local development projects to determine levels of community involvement in terms of (i) numbers of local organisation, (ii) numbers of people active in them, (iii) numbers helping occasionally, and (iv) numbers using their services (Bell, 1992). It also looked at the cost-effectiveness of community development work, showing for example that one hour of community development practice could produce 15 hours of volunteering.

Quantitative analysis of community and voluntary activity was now beginning to gather momentum. CDF and other organisations in the community development field successfully made the point that regeneration programmes such as SRB should treat levels of community activity with the same status as the more familiar indicators on housing, jobs and amenities.

The methods used in these Sandwell studies drew on the EFILWC research, with some modifications. Whilst there are now numerous surveys of local community activity taking place, we know of few which have used the 'full' EFILWC method, that is a survey of local community organisations paralleled by a statistical household survey. A method of this kind is, however, being used in five local 'demonstration projects' launched by the Active Community Unit of the Home Office in 1999. In one important respect the approach developed in Sandwell goes further than both the EFILWC and other studies in that it interprets the information in terms of what forms of community development the localities therefore need.

Resource Seven: Assessing the Strengths of Networks

The significance of networks

Networks can provide a significant contribution to ability of communities to take lead roles in regeneration and community development initiatives. Ideally, any assessment of community strengths should include an understanding and analysis of the place and role of local networks. Networks have been described as 'including associations, movements and coalitions ... semi-formal groupings in which each member organisation remains autonomous in its activities, but where enough common ground exists to establish shared agendas' (Eade and Wilson quoted in Skinner, 1997, p. 91). Because they are only semi-formal it means that different networks may serve different purposes and operate with different styles. On the whole however, most networks will play at least one and probably several of the following roles:

- the exchange of information

- joint working on issues of common concern

- co-ordination of activity so as to avoid duplication

- the exchange of skills and learning

- providing support and confidence to members

- developing a sense of common purpose

- providing an opportunity for debate and the development of collective views and possible action.

(Based on Gilchrist, 2001)

Assessing networks

The questions checklist in Resource One includes some basic questions on the role of networks, and the workshop notes in Resource Five described an introductory exercise. We expand on these here. This fuller list will be useful when the community strengths profile needs to be developed to focus more thoroughly on the role of networks. It may be that existing networks are perceived as blocks to progress, in which case an assessment of their role would be particularly useful. This would need to be carried out in close liaison with the network itself, involving the relationship building and liaison described in Part Two, Stage One, p. 22 above.

Networks can be assessed in broadly the same way as community groups and support organisations, through a:

- survey which profiles their role and strength in terms of organisation, skills, equality and involvement

- workshop exercise as outlined in Resource Five.

Workshops are a good way of identifying the strengths of networks because they ensure a range of perspectives is contributed. The very nature of networks means there may well be a divergence of views on the benefits of the network.

Below is a checklist of the kinds of questions that might be asked of networks. These can be used and adapted to either a survey or workshops. In either case we suggest you carefully pilot the questions chosen on a small sample group first to ensure the questions chosen will achieve what you intend to carry out.

BUILDING ORGANISATION

Has the network got a clear purpose?

How are members and contacts consulted about the network's purpose and effectiveness?

Does it have a defined membership – what are the boundaries of membership?

Does the current membership reflect the purpose?

What have been the achievements of the network over the last year?

What has hindered the network's development?

What would help the network function more effectively in the future?

What resources does the network have?

Is there a need for greater resourcing and if so what?

How often does the network review what it is doing?

BUILDING SKILLS

Is there a need for training or sharing of skills to help the network itself function effectively – if yes, what?

In what ways does the network identify the training needs of its member groups and organisations?

Does the network identify these training needs to support organisations, i.e. does the network see itself as having a strategic role around skills development?

Does the network itself provide training and learning opportunities?

Does the network itself provide support for its members or others?

Does the network itself base its work and activities on community development principles?

BUILDING EQUALITY

How does the network promote equality – what is the range of members involved, do they reflect different perspectives etc?

Are members supportive of new networks emerging to meet different needs?

Are there any gaps in representation of active members?

Do all members feel some ownership of the network?

Do all members contribute to the network's activity?

Do all members benefit from being part of the network?

How does the network avoid exclusivity and the development of cliques?

BUILDING INVOLVEMENT

How many members/contacts are active in the network?

Are the operating procedures of the network transparent?

Does the network play a role in influencing policy?

If yes, does it do this in an accountable way? If yes, how?

Is the network recognised and valued by lead agencies and partnership bodies?

Does the network enable people to 'connect' outside of the formal network? Does the network help to build links across boundaries of geography, theme or sector?

Resource Eight: Further Help

Relevant training courses and tool kits

> **Identifying Needs and Community Profiling**

The course sessions look at the first steps community workers need to take to get to know a community, its resources, strengths, needs and aspirations. The module includes:

- the concepts of community profiling and needs surveying

- why groups need to undertake profiles

- how to carry out effective consultation with local people

- the issues around inclusion and exclusion within communities, including the needs of minorities and disadvantaged groups

- the different research methods, data analysis, presentation of your findings, monitoring, and evaluation techniques and why to use them.

Practical work outside the training sessions includes:

- negotiating with a group to take part in a community profile

- working with a group to plan and carry out a survey/profile

- designing a community profiling exercise.

The module leads to the following awards from the Open College Network; 2 credits at levels 2 or 3.

For more details contact: The Community Work Training Co., 128 Sunbridge Road, Bradford BD1 2AT.

> **The Neighbourhood Initiatives Foundation** run several courses which include useful skills in profiling and analysis. These include: Planning for Real, Evaluation for Real, Community Needs Analysis, Introduction to Facilitation Skills. All courses include a manual around the subject area and some include a tool kit.

For more details contact: Neighbourhood Initiatives Foundation, The Poplars, Lightmoor, Telford, TF4 3QN.

> **Working with Community Organisations: a course for people working in communities**

This course is aimed at experienced community activists and paid practitioners. It typically involves 5 days teaching/facilitation plus assignment work through which participants can reflect upon their learning. Accreditation is offered through the

University of Leeds and the University of Birmingham (the course can form a module at undergraduate and postgraduate levels).

For more details contact: Federation of Community Work Training Groups, 4th Floor, Furnival House, Furnival Gate, Sheffield, S1 4QP.

> McCabe, A. Lowndes, V., Skelcher, C. (1997). *Partnerships and Networks – do they measure up?* York Publishing Services/Joseph Rowntree Foundation, York. This is an evaluation and development manual containing methods and exercises for assessment and recording of particular issues in the operation of networks and partnerships.

> Russell Gibbon and Alain Thomas, with assistance from Alan Twelvetrees: 'Evaluating Community Projects, new options with the 'percentagemeter''; Unpublished draft available from CDF Wales, Keepers Cottage, Llandarcy, Neath, West Glamorgan SA10 6JD

> Compass – The Community Profiling Software, Version 1 update. Leeds Metropolitan University.

COMPASS is a software package designed to enable people to conduct social audits or community profiles in their local areas. It helps with questionnaire design, data processing and analysis.

For further information contact: Policy Research Institute, Bronte Hall, Beckett Park Campus, Leeds Metropolitan University, Leeds LS6 3QS.

Useful organisations

ACRE (Action for Communities in Rural England)
Dean House, Somerford Court, Somerford Road, Cirencester GL7 1TW
Tel: 01285 653 477

ACW (Association of Community Workers)
Baliol Youth and Community Centre, Longbenton Methodist Church, Chesters
Avenue, Newcastle-upon-Tyne N12 8QP
Tel: 0191 215 1880

BASSAC (British Association of Settlements and Social Action Centres)
1st Floor, Winchester House, 11 Cranmer Road, London SW9 6EJ
Tel: 020 7735 1075

CDF (Community Development Foundation)
60 Highbury Grove, London N5 2AG
Tel: 020 7226 5375

Community Matters
12–20 Baron St, London N1 9LL
Tel: 020 7837 7887

FCWTG (Federation of Community Work Training Groups)
4th Floor, Furnival House, 48 Furnival Gate, Sheffield S1 4QP
Tel: 0114 273 9391

Forum for Community Work Education (N. Ireland)
3rd Floor, Philip House, 123/137 York Street, Belfast BT15 1AB
Tel: 01232 232587

SCCD (Standing Conference for Community Development)
4th Floor, Furnival House, 48 Furnival Gate, Sheffield S1 4QP
Tel: 0114 270 1718

SCDC (Scottish Centre for Community Development)
Suite 329, Baltic Chambers, 50 Wellington Street, Glasgow G2 6HJ
Tel: 0141 248 1924

WCVA (Wales Council for Voluntary Action)
Llys Ifor, Crescent Road, Caerfilli CF8 1XL
Tel: 01222 85 5100

Bibliography

Barr, A. and Hashagen, S. (2000a) *ABCD Handbook A framework for Evaluating Community Development* (London: Community Development Foundation)

Barr, A. and Hashagen, S. (2000b) *Achieving Better Community Development: Trainers' Resource* Pack (London: Community Development Foundation)

Barr, A., Hashagen, S. and Taylor Peter (2000) *Working with ABCD Experience, Lessons and Issues from Practice* (London: Community Development Foundation)

Bell, J. (1992) *Community Development Teamwork: Measuring the Impact* (London: Community Development Foundation)

Bell, J. (1999) *Doing Your Research Project: A Guide for First Time Researchers in Education and Social Science* (Buckingham: Open University Press)

Burns, D. and Taylor, M. (2000) *Tools for Auditing Community Participation – An Assessment Handbook* (Bristol: The Policy Press/Joseph Rowntree Foundation)

Burton, P. (1993) *Community Profiling – A Guide to Identifying Local Needs.* (Bristol: University of Bristol)

Chanan, G. (1992) *Out of the Shadows: Local Community Action in the European Community* (Dublin: European Foundation for the Improvement of Living and Working Conditions)

Chanan, G., Garratt, C. and West, A. (2000) *The New Community Strategies: How to Involve Local People* (London: Community Development Foundation)

COGS (2000) *Active Partners: Benchmarking Community Participation in Regeneration* (Leeds: Yorkshire Forward)

COGS (2000a) 'Annex 2A Framework for Measuring the Progression of Developing Local Communities' (unpublished) (South Yorkshire Objective One Programme Priority 4)

Commission for Racial Equality (1995) *Racial Equality Means Quality; A Standard for Racial Equality for Local Government* (London: Commission for Racial Equality)

Community Business Scotland Network (2000) 'Community Economic Profiling - Information Pack' (West Calder: Community Business Scotland Network)

Dale, P. and Humm, J. (2002) 'Neighbourhood Baselines for Capacity Building' (unpublished) (London: Community Development Foundation)

Department of the Environment, Transport and the Regions (1997) *Involving Communities in Urban and Rural Regeneration: A Guide for Practitioners* (London: DETR)

Department of the Environment, Transport and the Regions (2000) *New Deal for Communities Race Equality Guidance* (London, DETR) and see also www.regeneration.dtlr.gov.uk/consult/newdeal/race

Department of the Environment, Transport and the Regions (2000a) *Preparing Community Strategies* (London: DETR)

Gilchrist, A. (1995) *Community Development and Networking* (London: Community Development Foundation)

Gilchrist, A. (2001) 'Strength Through Diversity: Networking for Community Development' (unpublished) (Bristol: School for Policy Studies, University of Bristol)

Harris, V. (ed.) *Community Work Skills Manual* (Bradford: ACW/CWTCo.)

Hawtin, M., Hughes, G., Percy Smith, J. (1994) *Community Profiling – Auditing Social Needs* (Buckingham: Open University Press)

Lloyd, P. et al (1996) *Social and Economic Inclusion through Regional Development* (Brussels: European Commission)

Passey, A., Hens, L. and Jas, P. (2000) UK Voluntary Sector Almanar 2000 (London: NCVO)

Skinner, S. (1995) *Directories and Resource Guides: How to Produce Them* (London: Community Development Foundation)

Skinner, S. (1997) *Building Community Strengths: A Resource Book on Capacity Building* (London: Community Development Foundation)

Social Exclusion Unit (2000) *National Strategy for Neighbourhood Renewal: A Framework for Consultation* (London: Cabinet Office)

Social Exclusion Unit (2001) *National Strategy for Neighbourhood Renewal: Policy Action Team Audit* (London: Cabinet Office)

Social Exclusion Unit (2001a) *A New Commitment to Neighbourhood Renewal: National Strategy Action Plan* (London: Cabinet Office)

SCCD (2001) *Strategic Framework for Community Development* (Sheffield: SCCD)

Taylor, M. (1995) *Unleashing the Potential: Bringing Residents to the Centre of Regeneration* (York: Joseph Rowntree Foundation)

Wates, N. (2000) *The Community Planning Handbook* (London: Earthscan)

Wilcox, D. (1994) *Guidelines for Effective Participation* (Partnerships Online) and see www.partnerships.org.uk/guide

Feedback Form

We'd like to hear from you! If you use the Assessing Community Strengths approach, please let us know. It would be helpful to know how you got on, and any ideas you might have on how the approach could be developed further. This information will be passed on to the authors too. You can email us, or write to the address below, describing your experiences of carrying out a community strengths assessment.

Also, if you'd like our publications to be more effective for community development and participation, we'd really appreciate any comments you have on this book. Do also visit our website at **www.cdf.org.uk** and click on 'Publications' if you are interested in any other titles we publish.

If you'd like to comment, please photocopy the form and fill it in, write us a letter, or email a response to:
CDF Publications, 60 Highbury Grove, London N5 2AG.
Fax: 020 7704 0313; Email: admin@cdf.org.uk

What I like most about this handbook is:

What I like least about this handbook is:

What I found most useful about this handbook is:

What I found least useful about this handbook is:

Ideas for future CDF publications are:

Your name:

Position: Organisation:

Address:

                                             Postcode:

Tel: Email:

Date: